In memory of my mother, grandmother and Aunt Tanya

Dedicated to my husband

QUALIFYING

In Law and Life - The Journal

CONTENTS

INTRODUCTION

"This journal is simply a record of pursuing my desired aim. It serves as a record to monitor my thoughts through the journey I have chosen for the future. Whatever happens from recording this journey, whether the goals transpire or not, is probably secondary. It is more about finding out myself, how to deal with life and embarking on journey of growth from paralegal to qualifying as a lawyer and beyond. If you think you want it now, truly think about what else you are likely to want in the future as you evolve.

If you think you know what you want, you will never actually know until you have it. It is only when you see your dreams in reality, in light of the good, the bad and the ugly that you realise dreams are merely happy delusions to get you through the journey of life."

ABOUT THE AUTHOR

I was born in a third world country and lived in relative economic poverty. I was raised by grandmother until I moved to the UK. I moved to the UK to be with my mother in my early teenage years. My father was absent for the most part of my life. Despite the odds, I studied law and pursued a career in the legal field.

I recorded my journey of pursuing a career in law to qualify as a lawyer through a series of journals. My journals reflect the highs and lows that life has brought to me. In my journals, I explore my identity through analysis of family dynamics, socio-economic disadvantage and the inextricable link to qualifying as a lawyer. My journey to self-discovery connects my past and present to future aspirations.

This is a publication of my journals from years 2015 to 2020. It is an honest account of events that occurred in my life in the process of qualifying. I explore fleeting thoughts and emotions captured at the centre of my experiences as it happens, in a manner written unapologetically.

PART 1

Pre-Qualifying

1. THE PARALEGAL YEARS

31 August 2015

Can opener – added to the basket. As I finalised my online order, I reminisce my awkward encounter with the new guy I am dating, Luke. We started dating a few months ago and when I brought him back to my studio flat on one occasion, he helped himself to preparing a meal in my small kitchen. Holding a can he asked, "where is your can opener?" I did not have one so I responded, "don't worry, I normally use a knife." He looked confused.

I moved into this small studio several months ago and I have been meaning to purchase essential items for the flat but have not had time to get around to it.

I took the can from Luke's hands and I insisted, "here let me do it." I grabbed a knife and without any hesitation, proceeded to stab the can, opening it with strong force yet careful skill. Luke was surprised at my ability to open the can with a knife. He laughed. It was like he was dating a woman from the Amazon.

Although Luke and I have some similarities – we are both paralegals aspiring to become lawyers for one – and we are generally in the same wavelength in terms of our future for the most part, our backgrounds are from two different worlds. Luke may have known me for a few years before we started dating, but there are still so much he does not know about me.

I am hopeful that Luke and I will continue to get to know one another and that we will find happiness in our relationship. I hope to enjoy every single moment we have together. I am certain that the next few years will be nothing but pure bliss.

28 December 2015

The past four months were hectic. Unfortunately, all the support staff in my current job have been made redundant, including me. It was difficult to find myself in such an uncertain situation given I recently committed to a longer rental tenancy for a new flat. Luke and I decided to move in together. I took a week off to move my stuff and after a lot of frustration, Luke and I were able to lift our sofa up three flights of narrow stairs with a lot of struggle!

As I rested from lifting the sofa, I received a call from my manager. I was hopeful that it would be to say hello but how naïve I was. My manager explained that the role of support will be shifted to a new branch being set up in the north. She avoided the use of the word "redundancy" and said that I would be offered a job up north with less pay, but it was clear, my role along with other support staff were no longer available. I felt very sad and anxious. I loved my job – but I realised that businesses give when needed and take when they can. How will I be able to pay rent for my new flat?

Although Luke and I could both afford to pay our rent now, would we still be able to pay rent in the coming months? The worst thing is that we were not notified at all. The business seemed to be doing well and I can only think that the busines did this for more money. There was no consultation or indication that there will be a blanket policy of redundancy.   It did not matter if you worked well or not, your role was going. Why did I work so hard at this job? If I was aware earlier on perhaps I would stayed where I was and not moved to a new flat. But here I was, tired lifting the sofa having moved in to a new flat that I might not be able to pay rent for. It is possible that we could be lifting this sofa right back down quicker than we could lift it up the flight of stairs.

Whilst worrying about the imminent redundancy, I was also worried about my mother. My mother has unfortunately been in and out of hospital. She only went for a usual dialysis session but she was not released. Starting to realise she is becoming extremely weak. My mother has multiple medical issues with her kidney, heart, diabetes and she also has wound that looks so foul it could be narcotic. It is painful to watch my mother who had been so strong and determined, is no longer vibrant and ambitious having succumbed to the ailments of life.

I prepared my CV and applied to paralegal jobs in my field. Luckily, I found a job fairly quickly. I came cross a really good recruiter who managed to get me two interviews. A week from the redundancy announcement, I was able to secure four job interviews back to back. By the fourth interview, I was concerned I would get the name of the firm wrong as I had been jumping from one interview to the next. Thankfully, all interviews were fine. I had two job offers and before I can hear from the other two, I considered taking the first job offer. I was indecisive about which job to take. One offered more salary but possibly required work to be done in areas of law that I have not really thought of doing, whilst the other job paid less but focused solely in the field of what I wanted to do. I took the job that paid less but focused on the area of law I wanted to do. I figured that it was better to do what I love.

1 January 2016

I spent my Christmas with Luke and his parents. I spent the New Year with Luke and my family. The difference between each experience is vast. We are offered something to eat almost every half hour or so by Luke's parents. With my family, any feelings of hunger are superseded by our concerns over my mother's health deteriorating.

24 April 2016

I want to have control in my life. Nothing seems to be going as planned. I realise that my mother does not have long to go. After five months of my mother going back and forth in ICU, the doctors have now confirmed that unfortunately, there is no treatment that can cure my mother. My mother will now be undergoing palliative treatment. The doctors said this to me in front of my mother. My mother was a nurse and therefore, she would have fully understood all of the terminologies mentioned so she knew exactly what this means. I would have preferred if the doctor did not say this in front of my mother. I could see that my mother was devastated. It is a fight that she cannot win and although I wanted her to keep fighting, I could see she felt it was no longer a fight that was worth fighting for. This was deeply upsetting. I would have preferred if my mother could at least be allowed to think that there was hope of her getting better.

I continue to visit my mother in hospital. Although I have seen her health deteriorate gradually in the last few months, it sometimes still shocks me how different she is physically and emotionally. Sometimes we have good days when she is herself. More often than not, there are bad days. Days when she would be so delirious because of medication that it was unbearable to see. There would be times when she would spew out her hatred towards my father. Even at her death bed, this hatred continues to rot in her heart worse than her narcotic wound. Pain lingered as neither wound seems to heal. I felt my mother's anguish as I imagined what she went through.

My father was a man who broke my mother's heart. Long before my mother's illnesses surfaced, her soul had already been ruptured by my father. My mother married my father, a respectable man. My father was an accountant by trade. He had no siblings and unfortunately his parents both passed away so he educated himself through sheer hard work. My mother had fallen in love with a man so worthy of admiration that she gave her world to him. Once married, they went travelling together to pursue their new life. After the honeymoon, my mother sat staring at my father's achievement – his education certificate was laid bare on their wall to be admired and so my mother cherished the brilliance of my father. She was at awe that she had been able to marry such an amazing man. It was almost too good to be true.

The sunlight hit my mother's eyes and she was almost blinded as she stared at my father's certificate. She squinted her eyes. The certificate did not seem to have the sparkle she was expecting.

Why is that? She looked closely at the certificate and the seal was not embossed. The seal looked printed. She compared the seal of my father's certificate to her own. Something is wrong. The seal is not authentic. My father's certificate slipped from my mother's grasp, the frame crashed and with it, my mother's dreams. The certificate confirming my father's achievement as a qualified accountant was a fraudulent document. He was a fraudster. This was the beginning of discovery she was about to make about the man she married.

My mother searched my father's documents and there she found telephone numbers with random names. She was convinced that she was right although she prayed she was wrong. She called the telephone numbers one by one asking how they knew my father. My father had siblings. He had parents. It was very surprising that my father lied about his family. Why would he do that? My mother phoned the last number. A woman answered. This woman did not just answer the phone, but she also answered her burning question. What is going on?

The woman on the other line was my father's wife. My father was already married before he met my mother. In fact they had children. The woman wanted to know who my mother was. Suddenly, my mother became aware that she was unknowingly my father's mistress. My mother was distraught – not just for her own sake, but for this poor woman on the other line who was expecting my father to return to her and her children. How does she explain that the husband they both married was a fraudster and a bigamist?

My mother's heartache did not stop there.

12 July 2016

I was pretty content in being a paralegal as long as I was in the field of law that I wanted. There was a part of me that wanted to just stay in a good paying paralegal role as it was comfortable enough. Luke encouraged me to apply - he said I should really be looking for a training contract. I shrugged it off and insisted that I was happy as a paralegal as there is less stress. Before all the headache of redundancy and my mother being sick, I enjoyed being a paralegal. I enjoyed drafting as many forms as I can and delivering tasks without having to worry about them once done. The responsibilities were left with the lawyers. As long as I did what I am told, I could go home and not worry about work.

However, I knew deep down Luke was right. I should stop hiding from my fears of pursuing my goal. I should at least try. It also dawned on me that my mother may never see my qualify as a lawyer unless I try. If my mother saw me qualify, perhaps she would be proud of me. So I applied for the role without telling Luke. I only told Luke when I was called in for the interview. I figured there was no point in telling him unless I was selected for an interview. I had to tell him at this point as he would notice when I prepare for it

Well, some good news – I managed to secure a training contract! I am excited about this. I need to plan so that I am making the best out of my experience. I will be joining a Legal Aid firm specialising in human rights. I have not done Legal Aid in practice so this will be a learning curve for me. On the plus side, I will be helping those who are most vulnerable.

How did I get this training contract? Well, remember when I was made redundant and I looked for a new job? I continued to receive notifications of job vacancies and I received notification for this role. I applied for the role, prepared for the interview, had a trial to and got the job! The great thing about high street firms is the ability to negotiate with the principal solicitor interviewing me. In corporate firms, I would have to go through a series of approvals from various people. In this case, I was able to get an indication of a positive result at the actual interview. It was an almost guaranteed promise of a training contract – not a maybe I will get a training contract but a definite yes! I will start as a caseworker for about a month and then once the training contract is registered with the SRA then I can call myself a Trainee Solicitor! I am due to start in August so I am still working for my current employer.

20 July 2016

I was hoping to get an early night today as tomorrow I have to sort out my mother's place. As she is still in hospital, I have to do a couple of things for her. Her place is about two hours one way from where I live so travelling back and forth is the tiring part. But, if I travel from work that means I will be travelling from central London so that my commute to my mother's place will only be an hour but coming back to my place would still be two hours. So that means I will be home very late. Plus, on Friday there is an office gathering after work. The next few days will be really busy. On the weekend, I will visit my mother in the hospital.

25 July 2016

Whatever happens, as of course there is no guarantee in life, I have already taken the majority of steps I could have taken to achieve my goals for this year. I feel absolutely ready for the training contract. Whatever I have on my list of goals, I can achieve these once small step as a time. Some of my goals may have bigger hurdles but with perseverance I can hopefully get there.

Today, I was called as a "star pupil" in my current employment. One of the partners were trying to guess a reported case to use in a representation for one of their clients but the partner could not remember what the name of the case was. She explained the main principle point of the case, the ratio decidendi (reason for deciding). Others were trying to guess but no one seems to get it right. The case sounded familiar. I let my thoughts drift to try and remember the name. Aha – yes! I remember the case. I guessed and it was right! Very pleased with myself.

Putting the compliment aside, it brings me joy to know I have a fairly good knowledge in the field I am in. I love what I do and I have been wanting be in this field of law for such a long time –

since before I started my degree in fact. I will continue to want to do this for the rest of my life. I did not settle for any type of field. I knew the field of law that I wanted and I pursued it. I have a travelled a longer journey to get here but doing what I love makes it so fulfilling. I find that the learning process is much more worthwhile than chasing after title or money faster. My interest and passion for the field of law that I am doing has developed and grown over the years. I wanted it so much then and I have been loving every moment of being in this field.

30 July 2016

I only have one day off this week and between work, family and friends I feel exhausted. I have to regain my strength tonight. I want to prepare for my new job. I have to be able to absorb information quickly and stay clear of emotions relating to personal and family problems. It is very hard to do this but I must remain firm and strong. I must remain professional and put the emotional feelings I have to one side. I have to start transitioning my mindset to the new role.

3 August 2016

Today is my last day in the city. I will be working at the new job tomorrow. It has come around quickly. I am slightly anxious about starting a new job but I am hopeful that my first day will be a good start of a new chapter.

2. TRAINEE SOLICITOR

5 August 2016

I have already started my new job. I was given tasks regarding an appeal and Judicial Review. Today, I am seeing a client. All is well apart from the journey to work. My commute is about an hour and half. I need to settle down to a routine. I need to work on managing physical case files, connecting with clients and colleagues, having a checklist for different types of applications and being knowledgeable in my line of work.

It is 11:30pm. Today, we had a few hours training regarding application process for human rights claims. Some of the areas mentioned were new to me. I learnt a few things and it is also quite nice to be able to sit down with others in a round table and learn together.

I also met with a client today. I prepared the checklist that my supervisor needed to take instructions from the client only to realise that my supervisor was heading towards the door after I was introduced and I was in fact going to be taking instructions from the client directly. It was definitely a learning process. I was sweating so much and the nerves were kicking in. After a while, I became used to it and I quite enjoyed taking instructions. I feel proud that I was able to take instructions for just over an hour for an appeal with a tight deadline.

Some things that I have learnt about taking instructions.

Be prepared to sweat – a lot – especially during the summer if the air conditioning is not working.

If you ask a question, clients will not know the answer from memory. They will look at a pile of paperwork and chances are, they will not be able to find the answer. This could just be a waste of time.

Instead, go through the documents in front of them and ask them if any documents are unclear. For instance, what are the receipts for, who are the extra names on the document, etc. I found that after a close scrutiny of the documents, some of them were not useful because they were irrelevant.

Do not be afraid to ask for a timeline. Get the client to draw a timeline if their account of events do not make sense. Sometimes, the client is unclear when explaining it as they go back and forth. It may be helpful for them to see the details on paper. Also, if the client is not confident in English, it may seem that the client may contradict evidence but be patient and give client the benefit of the doubt as it may be harder for them to communicate.

Absorbing information from the documents (note that appeals can be document heavy) is a very important skill. Being able to do this quickly is a must. There must be a structured way to review the documents in order to be efficient. For instance, arranging the documents per person or per rule requirement as you go along.

Have all the forms ready. If the forms are not complete and the client needs to sign the forms, ensure the signature pages are one sided and have all correct information on each side because although the rest of the form is yet to be finalised, the signature pages are final. The one sided signature page will help in reprint of the form easier if necessary. If you can complete the forms electronically then that would be better. Similar principles apply to witness statements.

You can start preparing the basic details and research for Grounds of Appeal, but the background details can be amended once full instructions are taken.

Read, re-read, leave some time apart between drafting and finalising to get fresh perspective, write things down as you remember it and read again the Grounds of Appeal.

10 August 2016

Remember that I should try to be amenable to clients. If I want to say no to a client, I can offer to check with a supervisor, government body or another third party to see if possible. In reality, I know how the conversation is likely to go but at least it is supported by someone else so client less likely to take it personally.

12 August 2016

Not sure where I am finding the words to write the Grounds of Appeal. Even though there are times that it almost feels impossible to even start the work let alone finish the whole piece, when I think I have written enough and could not possibly write anymore, there they are – words – somehow pouring out from my thoughts, forming themselves through ideas after reading and re-reading the grounds I am challenging.

There are no shortcuts. After a careful start of the work, grappling with documents as thick as two pillows put together, figuring out the law and applying it to the current facts- assessing what the current facts are from pieces of information from documents scattered here, there and everywhere – it is truly a wonder how lawyers can do this regularly. Then there is the completion of the work as drafting is not enough. The draft must be proof read for spelling, grammar and factual errors. The amendments would be made from proof reading but it is not finished yet, it must have a final check for factual inconsistencies and anything that can jeopardise the case. This means more reading and further checking.

18 September 2016

The forms to register my training contract (officially called Period of Recognised Training) were sent to the SRA. It was sent a week ago. There are so many things occurring this week. Today alone will be very busy.

Apart from work, I am thinking of the following things. Discharge of my mother from hospital. Conveyancing instructions for the flat Luke and I want to purchase. For now, I need to focus on tasks in front of me. Make sure I take adequate breaks and keep my motivation upbeat.

26 September 2016

I am officially a Trainee Solicitor and I am loving it. I am loving the title and the work it entails. I am so glad I am training in the field I set out to achieve. I do not mind if the journey has taken longer, I am finally here.

I am refining my skills, absorbing information, drafting representations, client skills and many others. I love this field of law and this is what I want to do for the rest of my life. For the first time, in a very long time, I feel successful.

27 September 2016

I am coming home late again from work but it does not matter. I enjoy what I do. Every single part of it. I love the research part and I am learning so much about the process. However, I do need to organise my files a bit. I must spend about ten minutes each day organising my files.

I must also start looking into writing articles. I should confer with my colleagues first.

I should consider becoming more refined. I need to start acting and thinking like a lawyer. I should observe how lawyers act. I am in the legal field and I am making it happen. My hard work is starting to finally pay off. I have finally reached a level that I can consider to be a basic standard. I definitely have a lot more to work on but I am getting there.

I am also trying to buy a property with Luke in the meantime. Hopefully that will come through so I can live close to work. That means I can get to work sooner or stay later at work.

28 September 2016

Today, I won my first human rights appeal! I am so thrilled! Words

cannot describe this feeling! I want to remember this feeling forever! I want to help clients like this again and again, forever! The
case was privately funded as it had been assessed to be low merits
so Legal Aid was not appropriate. But despite the low chances, I
am pleased to say the appeal was granted! I remember the preparation of bundle and how I prepared the client for the hearing.
I have taken a mental note that this is how I should conduct my
next appeals. Definitely very pleased today and so heart-warm-
ing.

3. THE STRUGGLE

1 May 2017

Autumn of last year has been so intense sometimes I could not even find the words or energy to write.

Amongst the hardest situations in the last year, I think this one really pierces my heart. When I was studying for law, my mother would ask me endlessly about my training contract. She would ask if I will be able to get the training contract so coveted as the holy grail for all lawyer hopefuls. Although I never explained to her that I struggled to even get experience in the legal industry let alone a training contract, I think deep down she knew. She once offered to approach law firms for me for a training contract as I shook my head explaining that is not how it works.

I finally secured a training contract. I was elated as I told my mother. I even showed her my business card confirming I was now a Trainee Solicitor. Unfortunately, this day was not a good day for my mother. She was not herself as the medication has really affected mind. I know that it was not her when she dismissed the news I have told her, tossing my business card to the floor. I know it was the medication. But it is still hurt. I thought that once I get a training contract, this was it and my mother would feel happiness. I thought that once I climb this mountain, this would be the top. But it does not feel like I have reached the top. With my mother's illness, it feels like I have an even bigger mountain to get through and I knew there was no way to make it to the next mountain. Money had no value. Achievement was meaningless.

Unfortunately, after a long period of terminal illness, my mother passed away on 17 October 2016. I last saw my mother in hospital. I was with Luke. It seemed that my mother was doing well as she managed to laugh at my predicament. My car broke down in the middle of a one way street and a police had to push my car to safety. I will never forget my mother's laughter. It was a faint laugh but it brought a smile to her face. She was in good spirits as I showed her the flat Luke and I were about to purchase. She looked at me in awe. It was if to say that she was proud of how I was getting along in life. I did not tell her that we were mostly using Luke's savings he initially saved for him to go to law school to put down as a deposit as she seemed so pleased. The nurse said that they were conducting x-rays and so we needed to leave. As a I said goodbye to my mother, I waved and walked off to embrace Luke. I did not realise that this was the last my mother will see of me, walking off with Luke, the only man she has finally approved of and the man I will soon marry.

For the funeral, I wrote a Eulogy. The first one during my twenties and the last Eulogy I can only hope to ever write.

"I will always remember my mother as a proud nurse, an obedient daughter towards my grandparents and a responsible sister to my aunts. To my brother and I, she is both a mother and a father – having given life and never failing to provide for us. As a child, she was hero. A fairy that returned with gifts. We missed her terribly when she was not around. Once reunited, we would take long naps with her in our lazy afternoons. As a child, hugging my mother was like hugging a warm pillow. The years somehow accelerated and we no longer had much time to spend together.

Time reversed the role of dependency at a premature and exceedingly fast rate. Suddenly, my mother's strength has become mine. My weaknesses and hers have become one and our personalities had an uncanny resemblance. My mother and I have both become synonymous to women of strength. Although it was hard at first to understand, my mother was actually trying to pass to us the knowledge of life. Whilst still in the process of reaching for the knowledge of life, a brief glimpse of death appeared around the corner.

Death was coming to pass; but surely, death will knock at someone else's door. The shadow of death has finally loomed and arrived at our front door. I heard his footsteps and I dared not make a sound. I was afraid he would knock and ask for my mother. I had to bargain with death; no medicine, no money – but just a rosary. God, I have not spoken to you in a long time. But please, if you could remember that I prayed to you as a little girl and I am still that little girl. I ask you, please save my mother.

I looked outside and death waited patiently, watching my mother in constant and increasing pain. Death felt my stare and he whispered, "Why are you so afraid? I have not come to take. I have only come to save." No. "Mother, you must stay here with us. Mother, if you hear a knock, please you must not let death in." I turned away for a moment, and the door swung wide open. Death knocked and my mother let him in. I ran to follow my mother until I could no longer catch my breath. My mother was cradled in the arms of death. For the first time, in such a long time, she looked comfortable. Now I understand, she wanted to rest in peace..."

My brother and I arranged my mother's funeral. It has been a year of surreal difficulty for my mother and all of us. The regular visits to ICU, physically and mentally draining. Seeing a loved one be in so much pain really strikes through the soul. Nurses and doctors speaking words that seem alien, almost feeling like they are all just talking at me as I stare in silence. Having to make life or death decisions with no right answers. Correspondences from debt collectors for my mother's unpaid bills. Feeling my own grief as well as carrying others. I saw, heard, felt and did what I had to do. I was present but to cope, was very distant at the same time. As much as we prepare for life, it seems nothing can truly prepare us for death. This part is one that has certainly changed my perspective on life.

After my mother's death, it was like I was lost in time and space. The emotional feelings were buried in work. There was no time for grief when I was in front of a client. Luke has been through all of it with me and he, my rock was showing signs of depression because of what I was going through. I had a training contract to think about so I had to push down the feelings. After work when I would come home very late in the evenings, the walk home was the perfect opportunity to let it all out. Just like a clockwork, as soon as there was nobody around, tears would just come pouring down my face. Sometimes I would walk slower in the dark so I can let out as many tears as I can. As I was also concerned about Luke seeing me in this state, my tears stopped in front of our place. I composed myself so Luke will never realise and thankfully, he did not. To me the walk home alone in the dark, was genuinely walking through darkness.

19 June 2017

I am halfway through my training contract. As part of casework with vulnerable children, I am required to undertake Level 2 IAAS accreditation and the exam is tomorrow. I spent four days studying – two days off work and two days during the weekend. I am feeling very anxious. In all of the exams that I have taken, I have always felt this way. I have to think positively. No matter what happens, I should not stop learning. Tomorrow is a small hurdle of what I have always wanted in my career.

20 August 2017

My work as a Trainee Solicitor has been going well. I was on my own in the last few weeks. My boss was on leave and my other colleague studying for exam. I enjoyed being in charge in the office for a bit. There were times when I would have to make decisions that have significant impact in people's lives. Now that my boss is back, I now have reassurance for any problems that I encounter.

27 March 2018

I must keep my goals focused. A year and half into my training contract and I need to maintain my motivation. Any self-improvement that I must do should be done but I have to bear in mind that life is about dealing with any problems. Whatever happens, I have to be able to deal with the stress.

I have five more months to go until I qualify. I will make the most of this period to really improve. I hope to transition from Trainee Solicitor to a fully qualified lawyer and these last months will be the transitional period.

I have everything that I need and I am in the processing of completing my goals. I should be thankful and grateful of what I have accomplished. There are some lacunas in my life which I cannot ignore but I have to take each day as it comes.

18 April 2018

I am nearly there. I must learn to maintain my files like I am already a qualified lawyer. I must think like I am already a qualified lawyer. I must transition to a lawyer. I am a lawyer. I am grounded so I can solve other people's problems as well as my own.

20 May 2018

I went to the gym yesterday and today. It felt great knowing that I burned off between 2,300 to 2,500 calories within this weekend. I really want to lose more calories this week. I will try to work out in the morning at least twice this week

25 May 2018

Here I am, three months and five more days until I qualify. I have passed my Financial Skills exam and I have my Advocacy for Professional Skills Course.

28 May 2018

I want to adopt the following rules in my life. Try to learn something from everyone. Do something nice for someone else. Do something nice for me. Dress up in my favourite outfits daily. Only buy things I love.

30 May 2018

My boss is away until 6 June so I am dealing with some of his clients in addition to my own work. Today I received a call from

As a child, I would also buy detergent soaps so I can hand wash my clothes. Once, my brother and I agreed to split the costs for a bar of detergent soap which was already divided into five sections. After splitting four between us, my brother and I argued about the fifth bar of soap. I remember squatting in front of my bucket filled with laundry and bubbles, as my brother and I had a war about the last bar of soap. I threw a small garment soaked with water at him but he ducks so I miss. He threw a soaking pair of large jeans at me and of course, it hits me on the face. He roars with laughter and the more he found it funny, the more I became infuriated. My brother was a giant for his age. He was only a few years older than me but he looked like a full blown sumo wrestler. I on the other hand, was a very small girl. Sometimes, I did my best to punch and kick him but all my efforts were comical as all my brother had to do was put his arm out and my tiny arms could not reach him.

In the market, we could not afford to pay to use the public toilet so I was in charge of disposing our family's sanitation waste. To be perfectly frank, my grandmother used a bucket to urinate and at the end of the day, I would carry the bucket filled with urine away from my flailing arms, careful not to splash any on me. I discovered the hard way that there was no proper facility to dump such sanitation waste so it had to be done discreetly. I remember that one occasion when I had been so naïve and following my grandmother's instructions, I dumped the urine by the water tap where fish mongers and butchers came. One lady asked me what I was pouring out. I innocently said the truth and also revealed my grandmother told me to dispose of it. I was told off by the lady. I came running back to my grandmother with the bucket still full. I explained what happened and my grandmother was dismayed. In a passive aggressive manner, my grandmother threw the contents of the bucket in front of the market. The next morning, the whole market reeked of urine. I was so embarrassed and from then on, I knew to dispose of the bucket waste discreetly.

We would spend the majority of our time in the market if we are not in school. On one occasion, my brother suggested that we go home to watch some television. We knew that we were supposed to look after the shop so this would never be allowed. My brother suggested we sneak away for a few hours and said no one would notice. My brother and I left the shop and walked home happily. Half way home, it started to pour down with rain. There was nowhere to seek shelter. We could either go back to the market soaking wet or go home. My brother suggested we go home so we can change our drenched clothes. I was only ten years old and my brother a few years older. Between the two of us, we realised that we did not have a key to the house so we had no choice but to return to the market soaking wet. My brother hid well from my grandmother.

Unfortunately, I was caught and given a good hiding. As punishment, I was made to stand in front of the market under the pouring rain. I am not sure what poured down faster on my cheeks, tears or the rain. Words went around the market quickly enough as people starts to talk. Thankfully, my Aunt Tanya came and saved me from further humiliation. Aunt Tanya took me by the hand, scolded me ever so slightly but she dressed me up in dry clothes. I was sobbing my heart out. I would like to think my grandmother felt bad for that. My grandmother grew up in the times of Japanese invasion and so she had a tough upbringing herself. I think deep down my grandmother did not think I was really going to keep up the punishment. She probably thought I would come back in the shop. Looking back, I think I stood there because I thought I deserved the consequences. I was only ten years old but I thought that if I did something wrong, I had to be accountable for my actions so if this was part of it then so be it, I can see it through.

My grandmother would pack lunch so we have something to eat in the market. As we did not have a fridge to store the food, ants would sometimes crawl in our food. Having a radio, a light and a fan in the market would have been considered luxury. We did not even have a phone so to speak to my mother from overseas, I had to go to our neighbour's house. Anyway, on one occasion in the market, our food had ants crawling through it but we could not afford to throw it away. I was told to pick out the ants and so I picked out as many as I could with my tiny fingers. Growing up in a third world country, I realise that my childhood was different. Not only different from those of my school friends in the UK, but also from my school friends in my country of birth. My school friends generally did not live a life in the market. They could go home from school and watch TV. The majority of my friends had parents, at least a dad that provided financial support and a mother to look after their day to day well-being. I knew my life has always been that bit more difficult from others so I was always hungry to improve my circumstances.

This November, I hope to return to my country of birth, to return to my life that was left behind and remind me where I had come from with hope that I can move towards my future with ease.

3 September 2018

Today is the day when my name will hopefully be listed on the Solicitors List. I have a whole day of waiting. I just have to think of other things to distract me in the meantime.

It is now 10:52pm. I tried to distract myself for most of the day. I saw clients to take instruction for their witness statement for the most part of the day. The best distraction is interacting with clients. I found that time flew by. Whilst with a client, I realised that it was 15 minutes before the roll was to be published. I could not focus so I asked the client to have a break.

It felt like the longest 15 minutes of my life. I thought about how long I waited to become a lawyer. I thought about the moment that my grandmother said to me she can see me as either a doctor or a lawyer. I was never good with blood and I was innately clumsy so being a doctor was never really an option. I thought about all of those times I wrote in my diary that one day I could be a lawyer.

I thought about the moment when I attended a career's fair to support my friend and got to talking to a law professor who suggested that I should try to apply for a law degree. Although I was sceptical given my subjects in A-levels were mostly art related and I had already missed the deadline for UCAS application for that year, somehow I managed to secure a place through clearance so I did not have to wait the following year. As I had made such a last minute decision, my accommodation was not arranged and I had very little money.

I remember during my third year in university, my mother was hospitalised so I stayed with my mother and did my coursework in the hospital. My laptop overheated on my lap but luckily I had it fixed so I did not lose my coursework and I could persevere with finishing it. As I went home to pick up fresh clothes for my mother, I cried with frustration from the pressure I was under – in hindsight, this seems to have become a habit that I somehow picked up again after my mother passed away.

I remember the careers advisor that I spoke with at university. With two more exams to go, I was concerned I could either get a 2.1 or a 2.2 grade depending upon how I study in the next few weeks. I knew that I had to get at least a 2.1 as most firms looked for this minimum grade when assessing training contract applications. The advisor suggested I stop focusing on the subject I enjoy and focus on my weaker subject. Thank goodness for this advice as otherwise, I would have done the exact opposite.

I thought about law school and the jobs I took to get legal experience with very little pay. I remembered having two jobs whilst studying at university full time – one was at WH Smith and the other volunteering at Citizens Advice Bureau. I remembered once I competed law school taking on my first job and leaving my mother's house with a mere £500 savings. My details did not reach payroll with my new job in time for me to be paid for the month so I had to pay rent and live with very little for the first few months.

I refreshed the web page. There it is - my name is on the Roll of Solicitors. I am a qualified lawyer! After a lot of hard work and dreaming about this for about 15 years, it finally happened today. I want to remember this moment forever. I am so incredibly happy.

4 September 2018

My first day as a Solicitor!

I don't feel like a Solicitor yet as I am still doing pretty much the same tasks as before. I am still the same person as before (but a very happy person) qualified and waiting for my practising certificate. Wonder when I will start to feel like a lawyer.

16 September 2018

Any big event for me is a delicate balance between celebration and grieving. Last month, I celebrated my birthday and qualifying as solicitor. I am also due to get married soon. I am fully aware that next month is the two year death anniversary of my mother.

As a lawyer, I am filled with happiness but yet feel sad that my mother did not make it to see this day. At least my close family and friends have made this last month special.

For my birthday last month, Luke surprised with me a trip to Paris. It was the first time I had taken the Eurostar to get to France. I had an amazing time visiting museums. I saw the Mona Lisa and Venus de Milo in the Louvre. I mostly saw the crowd and very little of the actual Mona Lisa painting but it was a great experience. I have never had so many steaks and wine. Luke really went all out during this trip.

My colleagues also surprised me with a cake at work. I was busy typing away when the lights were suddenly switched off. Then from a corner, I see my colleagues, including my support staff giggling away with a candlelit cake as they sang Happy Birthday to me - they have all been amazing and I treat them like family.

I also celebrated my birthday by having lunch with some of my family including my brother and cousin, Maria along with Luke and his parents. It was the first time that my family and Luke's family had all gathered together. My brother and cousin symbolise the only immediate family I have left and so this was also a way to introduce my family and Luke's family before the wedding in November. Luke's parents were obviously in an older generation than my brother and cousin. My family and Luke's family were different, not that there was anything wrong with that but admittedly, it was a type of generation that would probably not happen to casually meet in ordinary circumstances but were not for Luke and I being together. As such, I appreciated that they all made an effort to come.

I also had dinner with my close friends and they showered me with gifts. It was the first time I had pulled some of my close friends together for a meal to celebrate my birthday, including my friend Charlton whom I have known when I was a teenager. It was nice for all of them to be present. Whenever I am with family and friends, I am humbled. I am reminded that I am still the same silly person I have always been.

I sincerely believe that the world is my oyster. In the next decade, I hope to have a family of my own – one that I missed out on as a child having been looked after by my grandmother. Whatever happens in my life, whether or not my plans transpire, I must remember that I have a lot to be thankful for. The girl from the market has come so far. I am now a woman in a safe position of achievement, sufficient to secure a decent future with enough challenges to humble me.

19 September 2018

My practising certificate has finally arrived! I am a lawyer and I am starting to feel like one.

23 September 2018

It is 3:55am on a Sunday. I seem to have problems sleeping.

It is now 4pm. My cousin, Maria called me. She said she was concerned about my brother and wants me (his younger sister) to set him straight.

Firstly, my brother has never really listened to me. Secondly, he has never really listened to anybody telling him off. Thirdly, my brother and I have been through difficult times in different ways. As children without much parental supervision, perhaps he felt that his friends are like his family. We grew up not having a father. We grew up knowing our father was a fraudster and a bigamist – that he took advantage of others including my mother and justice was never served.

I remember when I was about ten years old and my brother only a few years older, a random classmate asked me if my father was a pilot. I was confused. Why would he ask this? It turns out, my brother had been going round telling everyone at school that my father was a pilot. I clarified that my father was not a pilot. He then asked what he did for a living and I said, "I don't know. He left us when I was very young." The boy was surprised, but understood not to ask further questions. I did not understand why my brother would make up lies like that. To me then, this was so typical of my brother. In hindsight, I realise that it was hard for my brother to accept the truth but could not bring himself to say it. In a weird way, perhaps my brother thought that pretending to have an ideal father would probably be just as good as having one. I do not understand fully but I probably understand it more than anyone else.

It is quite easy to point out my brother's mistakes, but it is a lot more difficult for others to put themselves in his position – that we came from a broken family. Anyone who had both parents from a young age will find it hard to understand the difficulty of not having a father - physically, emotionally and financially. The way that I see it, it is true my brother is less disciplined and he has gone astray in some aspects of his life, but I understand him for trying to bring some happiness in his life.

When a loved one is lost, things in life are devalued. Little things become insignificant. Life and living in the present becomes more important. For me, having arranged my mother's funeral, I saw life for what it was – a precious time that should not be wasted.

11 October 2018

Today, one of my clients wanted to take a photo with me. Although rather odd, it is flattering and I felt like a lawyer celebrity of some sort.

23 October 2018

I feel stressed about work. I thought that following qualifying, I would be able to manage my own time but managing all Legal Help, private client and some litigation, together with the new detention work is putting a lot of pressure on us.

24 October 2018

Today, it was my first time to attend IRC Brook House detention centre to advise detained individuals through legal surgery. Officially a qualified solicitor so people do take me seriously.

4 November 2018

Sometimes, when I watch dated movies I have slight concerns over portrayal of women in an overtly sexualised, objectified or of a weaker character. My concern is that I am aware that there is still a part of me that is impressionable so there is a possibility that I could subconsciously absorb this negative energy and apply it in my own day to day thoughts. I want to focus on my goals and for those goals to be of an important nature. If possible, I want to avoid the glass ceiling.

I am also writing an article for ILPA's Monthly. I am pleased about this. I will be getting my boss to review it. I will put both our names on the article as I want to share this opportunity with him

5. PAST AND PRESENT

16 November 2018

It is the day before my wedding. I am excited. I can't believe this day has finally come!

I have enjoyed planning this wedding. This was the first and most expensive party I have ever planned. It is almost like I have lived the wedding through my head so many times as I went through the process of planning. I enjoy the process of planning, most specifically trying to get value for money.

We wanted to save a lot of costs so we cut back where we could. With both Luke and I being in the legal profession and having met in a law firm, we decided to marry at The Law Society. The Law Society is a beautiful building and one that required very little decoration for the wedding ceremony and reception. Moreover, we could get a discount for the venue as I was a lawyer.

We planned for 60 guests to have appetisers, dinner and evening buffet. We have the whole venue to ourselves. We plan to have two violinists playing at the ceremony and partly during the reception. We cut back in costs with the following. Firstly my dress – I knew the design that I wanted and I found this at a discounted rate in a local wedding dress warehouse. I did my own makeup. I researched for professional wedding make-up and purchased the items I needed which would hopefully last for a long time, rather than one day. I did my own hair. I arranged flowers - the bouquets for me and my bridesmaids, the corsages and table flowers. I taught myself how to arrange this and ordered the flowers in bulk online. I made the wedding invites from blank cards and I also prepared the souvenirs. Although we had corkage for our beverages, it was still cheaper to choose that option rather than pay for the drinks per person. The bridesmaid dresses were suitable for a wedding but could also be appropriate as a day to day dress and these were ordered online. The rest were pretty standard such as the photographer, DJ, cake and so on.

We arranged for the honeymoon to be in my country of birth as Luke has never been and I have not been in over a decade. As I knew my way around my country of birth, I could find better deals for the honeymoon. I am looking forward to how everything turns out in the next few days. I shall sleep tonight and know that when I wake up, I am getting married!

18 November 2018

Luke and I are now married! The ceremony and reception went very well. I really enjoyed the day. Everyone was pleased with the venue and with the food. At the venue, I had quite a large room to myself and the bridesmaids to get ready in. The preparation in itself was a whole event already as it felt like we were having a daytime slumber party. We took a lot of selfies, had alcohol and I pranced around the room with my wedding dress barefoot. It was great fun. I intentionally arranged the drinks reception for the guests to arrive upstairs so that I can walk in and out freely downstairs if need be. Also, this means that Luke could do the majority of socialising with and thanking guests at the drinks reception - he is so much better with that as I find it all a bit awkward to be honest.

By the time the ceremony came, I already had a few to drink which was great as I was not as nervous when walking down the aisle. My maid of honour and bridesmaids walked down the aisle fist and although it was not rehearsed, it all occurred perfectly. I walked down the aisle on my own – unlike the tradition of the father giving away the bride, nobody gave me away and strangely, it felt just right. At this point, it is hypocritical for anyone to give me away since I have been walking through the journey of life on my own for a while. It was fitting that there was no one walking me down the aisle and I felt fine about it – either that or the alcohol I had consumed with my bridesmaids was in full force.

In the reception dinner, we decided that it was best to separate our table from family. This is because if we were going to have the traditional seating for parents near our table, my side would be lacking of parents and Luke was understanding enough that it was easier to just avoid this issue. Like many times in my life, I am now accustomed to glossing over the issues of parental absence – whether from parent meetings at school to wedding reception. It was the epitome of my life.

Luke made a speech, so did his best man, his father and my maid of honour. They all made great speeches and quite frankly, I was glad that I did not have to say a word in front of everyone.

I was very grateful to everyone for making an effort to come. Also, I was thankful to my friends for their support throughout. We organised it pretty well. I was pleased with it all and for the first time, I felt like a princess marrying my prince.

19 November 2018

I am currently on a flight with Luke. We need to catch our connecting flight from Hong Kong. I hope we can catch it. As Luke has never been to my country of birth and as I was pretty much broke for the most part of my studies and during my paralegal work, this was the only opportunity for me to take Luke to my home town. We planned to stay in the northern area a for week, visiting my hometown and head down south to explore some of the beaches.

21 November 2018

Luke and I went to visit my hometown. It took a while to reach it. We hired a driver to take us. The journey was slow, bumpy and hot, especially for Luke who has never experienced summer in November. As I had not returned to my hometown in over a decade, the driver was seriously doubting my ability to navigate through the roads where I lived before. I was convinced that I still possessed a level of familiarity through the roads that I had travelled on as a child. Sure enough, I recognised our house. Everything looked smaller - perhaps it was because I was smaller when I left.

The house was still the same but looked worn out through time. The house has been standing for over 60 years and probably was not renovated for about a decade ago. The bathroom and kitchen were last renovated over two decades ago. Parts of the roof were also collapsing and there is water damage in the ceiling upstairs. It seriously needed work to be done to it. I used to live in this house with my grandmother and brother. Now, my Aunt Tanya stayed here to look after it although with her illness, it really was not fair to expect her to do anything more than watch over the house. Aunt Tanya looked even smaller than I remember. I had not fully appreciated how much her illness has truly affected her until I saw her in person. She was really skinny and had lost her hair due to her dialysis. Her voice was also faint and she was generally quite frail.

Aunt Tanya is like my second mother. When my mother was overseas and I was looked after my grandmother, Aunt Tanya did for us what my grandmother and my mother could not do, especially since my grandmother was elderly and was barely literate. Aunt Tanya treated me like her own daughter which is why I treat her daughter, Maria like my own sibling. Aunt Tanya gave me notepads and materials for school. She would help write graduation speeches for me. She helped me memorise poetry in competition. She basically fulfilled the gaps of responsibilities that my grandmother and my mother could not do. She also encouraged me to take the entrance exam to SPED which is a special school for advanced students. She also took me to school despite the hours of commute every day. She also saved me from the further humiliation I faced when I was made to stand in the pouring rain in the market. It is not possible to recount every single effort she has done as she did so much.

I appreciated her time in welcoming Luke. I expressed that we will not stay very long as I did not want to take up too much of her time but that I will show Luke around the house. I could see she was frail and did not want her to feel burdened by our presence. I showed Luke around. Although I always thought our house was decent and perhaps it was when I lived there, walking around the house now, I could see why Luke would think that we lived below the standard from those living in the UK.

I expressed to Aunt Tanya that there was only one thing I wanted from the house and that is a photo album that I can take back to the UK, Although I cannot take back all photos, taking at least one album would be priceless for me.

Luke and I then visited the market. Just before I got out of the car, I saw my teacher from elementary school walked past our car window. I took a long look at her and was amazed as she did not seem to have aged a bit. It brought back memories of when I was in school when she brought out the best qualities in me. I answered her questions no other children could answer, spelt words only older children could spell and sold all the tamarind sweets I was allocated to sell. She gave me confidence in my ability and ranked me as her top student. I wanted to say hello to her, but something stopped me. I felt embarrassed. Strange how I would not have hesitated to say hello to her when I was a child but now as an adult I feel this way. The moment passed and it was too late for me to say hello.

The market looked a lot dingier than I remembered. My grand-mother's shop was closed. The market was darker than I remembered. The shop was covered with dirt and spider webs. I looked at the faded paint that was once so vibrant. The shop sign had a part of my initials. I think my grandmother thought I would be one of her grandchild that could one day help run the shop. I remembered how I used to open the shop and arrange the clothes. I observed every single nook and as far as I was concerned, I could open the shop now and arrange it back to how it was in exactly the same way. Even though the shop was dirty, there was a feeling of comfort from the familiarity of the market.

We walked around the market. I saw Uncle Martin, husband of Aunt Tanya. We briefly said hello. His shop is still very much the same as before, nearly over two decades ago. Uncle Martin is one of the few men that I respected when I was growing up. He actually taught me how to read and with his authoritative prominence, I learnt quicker out of worry of getting the answers wrong. When I was growing up, I thought of him as slightly stern and someone I would try not get crossed with me. As an adult, I realise he was simply a decent man who did a good day of hard work in the market and dedicated his life to his family.

Quite a few shop owners have died since I left the market. One shop owner called Leila also passed away. I really liked Leila. Leila was an elderly lady. When I was a child, I used to visit her shop and stay with her for a while when I was bored. She would tell me stories and I used to watch her use her sewing machine. She would tell me about her daughter who worked in Japan. She would also show me pictures of her daughter and I was mesmerised by her daughter's beauty. As I grew older, I understood from others that her daughter was working in Japan as an entertainer, with implications as a prostitute.

In the market, I walked past an empty corner. It used to have a stall of books for hire. There were only about less than a hundred books, mostly novels about romance. I remember renting books from this stall when I was a child. I was only ten years old but I could rent as much as I can and I made the most of it. I remember renting one book after another until I managed to read all the books available. The stall owner was not in a position to get any new books as this would mean travelling to the city, so I was sad that there were no more books to read. I am not surprised that the stall is no longer there as quite frankly, I was not aware anyone else rented books in the market.

I even saw the tap where I used to dispose my grandmother's waste bucket. It feels like the market has become even more crowded than it already was when I was there as a child. It is almost like every inch of the market is occupied by a stall or a person.

My husband stood in front of our shop sign – it was an odd vision, my husband Luke, towering in front of the shop where I once polished shoes using gas. I captured the moment by taking a photo, realising that the disparity from my past has now finally caught up with my present and my life has now come into a full circle.

22 November 2018

Today, Luke and I met my father. I decided to meet him as it is likely I may never see him again but I need to find answers why he did what he did.

Since my mother and father separated when I was about five years old, I did not know much about my father. I only knew what I was told. I searched for my father over a decade ago when I turned 18 years old. I was able to track my paternal uncle. Once I was able to find him, my uncle was very reluctant to let me contact my father. It was almost like my father did not want to be contacted. Eventually I was able to contact my father and invite him to my 18th birthday party. As I was growing older, I wanted to hear my father's side of the events that happened. I wanted to understand his view. I hoped that his version would explain and justify what he did.

The first time I properly met my father since he left us was before I turned 18 years old. I was outside a shop in my hometown. I was supposed to meet my father somewhere else but by pure coincidence, I was buying candles from a shop and he stood right next to me. I looked at him, recognising him from the photos I had. He looked different, obviously much older but I could tell it was him. He looked at me and I knew that for him, it did not even dawn on him that I was his daughter. Even though he knew that I was in town, to him I was a complete stranger. I introduced myself.

I was hoping my father would tell me it had all been a lie and that he was actually an accountant and that he divorced his first wife before marrying my mother. I also wanted to understand what happened after that. Despite my mother forgiving him to start over, somehow my father could not be faithful to my mother. In addition to the fraud and bigamy he committed, my father had an affair with our nanny. My mother was even supporting him financially. I wanted him to tell me that this was not true. I wanted him to tell me a perfectly valid explanation that could make my world make sense. To my surprise, my father confirmed that all of the events were true, with less anger than how my mother explained to me but the facts were pretty much the same. I was glad I found out the truth so I would stop imagining that my father was an angel and that somehow, I could magically justify what he did to reconcile with the belief that there is still good in this world.

To my father's surprise, I was able to recall very early memories as a toddler. Yes – I remember, even those moments he thought he was getting away with his extra marital affair, outside his already bigamist relationship, with the nanny. Seriously – what kind of a woman would have an affair with a married man so openly in the house that my mother paid for? They were both equally lacking in morals that they truly deserve each other. They now have children and I wonder how much their children truly know of what happened. What do the children think of their parents' shameful behaviour? I know I have carried this shame but have they? Do they realise that we were all borne out of a wrongful act and if my father had done the rightful thing, we really should not have been born?

I don't know what I was trying to achieve trying to reunite with my father. Did I want a relationship with him? I was glad he came to my party, even though he knew that my mother's family would hold resentment towards him for all eternity. I found him slightly paranoid and rather narcissistic. During his stay with us, he would question where I would go as he would be left by himself. If he must know, it is a hot country so I kept drinking water and hence I went to the toilet often. He was too worried about being left on his own with my maternal family's presence. Putting his pride aside, so far everyone in my mother's family had put on a brave face and gave him a warm welcome. Nobody in my maternal family has mentioned the things that he has done.

When I returned to the UK, I kept in touch with my father for a while. I thought that is what I should do. This was a way for me to experience having both parents like a normal person. One day, my father congratulated me for completing my law degree. I was grateful of course. Then I saw a comment he made on one of my Facebook photos. He said, "we made it!" Did we make it – together? My mother and I made it, yes – but my father? I realised that here was a man who liked to claim as his own things, title and achievement that he does not deserve because he has not earned it. How can he comfortably say that we made it? He was not there through what I have been through. In fact, his knowledge of how hard it was for me is so far off that the only way for him to get an idea of what it was like for me is if he somehow read my diary. From this point, I decided not maintain contact with him.

When my mother passed away, I received a series of messages from family friends and neighbours, mostly expressing their condolences. I noticed that my father managed to utter only one word to me, "condolence". Even my previous neighbours managed to say a few nice words about my mother but my father could not. My father could not bring to say more than one word to me. Perhaps I was grieving or maybe it was because I remember my mother in so much pain as she spewed out regrettable words in her deathbed about my father. Whatever it was, I called my father and expressed my feelings of resentment towards him. I did not hold back. I asked him why he has never apologised so sincerely.

My father started to apologise for what he did but with a qualification – that I should really forgive him because it was so long ago - that I cannot be mad at him forever. That is not an apology. I told him that changing my diapers when I was a baby is not enough to render him as a father because there is more to raising children to become an adult. I wanted to know why he did what he did. I demanded to know the answer. He never did answer. He did say that he had a heart problem and suggested I should be careful what I told him. The way I saw it, I should tell him sooner as I will not be able to tell him once he is dead. Speaking out was brutal - but fraud, bigamy and cheating with our nanny was worse and he was never legally held accountable to it.

Fast forward to two years later, I am now able to finally return to my country of birth. I decided to meet with my father to see if he can provide me with the answer I am searching for.

I told my father to meet me at the hotel we were staying at. I received a call that my guest was waiting at the reception. I looked at Luke with uncertainty – like I was bracing myself for what was about to happen. Luke comforted me and I felt reassured. I came down to the reception. I was so consumed of my emotions that I did not realise my father was impressed with the hotel we were staying at.

It was the best in the city – five star at its finest. The hotel had private jacuzzi in the rooms and had the full works of extravagance. My father can see that we can afford to splash out in sheer luxury. Even though I had come from the market and he had no idea that I have no desire of chasing money generally, for the first time I delighted in the fact that I can afford this so he can see I can afford the life he tried so very hard to obtain that he was willing to commit fraud over it. Yes – at my age, I was able to accomplish things no one in our family could, even without a father figure. I became a lawyer without him, I can afford this kind of indulgence and most importantly, I went through qualifying as a lawyer legally.

I showed him a photo album of the family I had taken from my grandmother's house. The photos in the album started from when I was a toddler until I was about eight years old. The album showed my father at the beginning, with some photos that were familiar as he had taken these himself. The photos in the album continued with my father abruptly disappearing from the photos. My father perused through the album, taking a glimpse of the moments he missed in our lives. It was almost like he watched us grow through the rest of the album. The album had annotations and comments full of happiness and love. My father asked if I arranged the album. He just does not get it. It was my mother that arranged the album. Despite what he did to her and our family, my mother treasured the very few good moments we had and arranged it in an album even including my father in the photos. She even wrote positive comments throughout. My father on the other hand, started a new life and pretended we did not exist.

My father made it clear. The reason why he committed fraud by pretending to be an accountant, faking his qualifications issuing fraudulent documents, pretending he was not married, that he had no family, abandoning his first family and kids behind, pretending that his parents were dead, committing bigamy, expecting my mother to support him and us financially and then cheating on my mother with the nanny - turning my life and my brother's lives upside down from the moment we were born until this very day was this – he wanted to be happy.

He wanted to be happy. Why did I question my whole world, my life and existence, when the reason was simple. He wanted to be happy to the detriment of our own – with complete disregard for law and integrity. There is nothing else to it and I can drive myself crazy searching for reasons to justify what he did. If justice was served under the law, he should have been jailed, but he got away with it with very little acknowledgment, reparation or remembrance as substitute. The sooner I accept that there is no justification for what my father did, the sooner I can move on with my life.

23 November 2018

After meeting my father, I knew I had very little energy to waste any more towards him. I had already exhausted my energy and emotions. Once he left, Luke and I had to make the most of our stay. I went for a massage. We looked around the city. Before we knew it, it was time to head towards our next destination which is down south.

Right now, we are waiting at the airport to take a flight to our next destination. I have put the meeting with my father in the back of my mind and I am very much looking forward to the next coming week.

We also received some great news this week. Luke managed to get a training contract! I am really pleased for him. He has worked hard and he deserves to qualify. There was a period when he felt down for a while due to uncertainty of his career. I am so happy and proud that my husband will be a lawyer!

24 December 2018

Honeymoon is over and back to work. My support staff has left. I have also informed my boss of my intention to look for a new job – although I am not obliged to - out of respect for him. I have sent out my CV and I am waiting to hear from potential employers.

I have been to the doctors and I found out that I have too much iron in my blood. I am also waiting to have an ultra sound to check my kidneys.

Since my mother passed away, I have a very different outlook on life. Before, I thought that all I had to do was be strong mentally and I can take on life. Now, I realise that life is more about enjoying each breath that we take, each taste, smell, music and vision that we see – life is about living and humanity is humbling.

I have achieved my purpose in 2018. Any forthcoming blessing in the next few decades are most welcome. I approach 2019 with peace and contentment.

6. CORPORATE OR HUMAN RIGHTS

3 January 2019

I have been looking for a new job and I am trying to secure interviews. I thought that I would not feel nervous about interviews now that I have qualified. Yet, I am still nervous about potential interviews. I still feel nervous even if I have some experience already.

I should just enjoy the ride really. I am in the best position of my career that I have ever been in. I still have a lot of potential. Of course, if I don't get the position, then it would probably be for the best not to get it rather than finding out it is a not a good fit down the line. I guess interviews are a chance to get an insight of what the firm is like.

I am really looking forward to the future. I have prepared a draft article for ILPA Monthly. I considered it more as a creative writing and different from the usual legal analysis that can be expected.

6 January 2019

It is Sunday afternoon. I am trying to practice interview questions. Even though I am now a qualified solicitor, I still fear rejection. I fear failure. I should not be afraid to fail. Whether or not I get this job, it will be a good practice for any other firms that I could interview with.

12 January 2019

I had two interviews yesterday. One was with ABC which is a human rights firm. In the afternoon, I had an interview with DE which is a corporate firm. I was offered a job at ABC on the spot. I said I will consider it and let them know. I keep thinking about the interview at DE. The questions asked keeps going through my mind. Even though I know that it is not possible for every single opportunity to be for me, there is something about potential rejection that can never sit well with me, whether I have a strong or little interest in it. I always seem to feel the need to achieve things that I try out for.

I know full well that the most important thing is that I tried. If I think about it closely, I was early in both interviews and I did what I could, resulting in at least one job offer on the spot. I guess this next job that I take will be the deciding factor whether I stay within the human rights sector or move on to the corporate world.

Although my career is at the most secure point it has ever been in, there is still a great amount of uncertainty about it. I suppose I had always envisaged that I would be working in the Legal Aid sector for several years. I made a promise to myself that I would help those in most need once I qualified. I guess when I look for a job with better pay in the corporate sector, perhaps it is greed driving me as I had forgotten about the promise I made.

In the corporate sector, I am aware that applications are mass produced. In human rights work, I feel that my skills as a lawyer are maximised, albeit the pay does not reflect it. I am more likely to achieve one of my goals of becoming a Solicitor Advocate if I worked in a human rights firm. There is uncertainty in both options and I have to be prepared for whatever comes my way. I am fully aware that as a qualified solicitor I should be earning more. However, I am not sure that I truly pursued law for money. My inherent characteristics were always innately close to a human rights lawyer. Looking back to my early diary, I already possessed a strong will to fight for social justice. I recall an extract from my diary when I was 13 years old:

"Sometimes, I regret being a girl. Well, my mum always rub it on my face. She says that I am a girl so I should clean the house, etc. But that's just sexist. Don't you just hate it when people are being prejudiced? If

I argue back, it is like I committed a crime. I'm supposed to be doing my art homework but right now I only feel like dreaming about the future. I am going to be a successful lawyer."

I can't believe I was 13 years old when I wrote this. Although 13 year olds are young, I find myself believing that even at such a young age, children are surprisingly very much capable of making a sound decision in life.

20 January 2019

It is a Sunday afternoon. I intend to work out, shower, then prepare for another interview. I obviously want to do my best. Although I have already accepted the job offer at ABC and it may actually make it easier if I do not get this job offer, I still want to do my best as it has already been arranged. I am thankful that I am in the best position possible. Of course, we can always do better – we can always find a better paying job. However, I think I am exactly where I wanted to be in life. As long as I am doing what I love, everything else in my career will follow. I am not perfect and it is not possible to get every single thing that I ask for so I am truly counting my blessings.

When I first started journaling, I had no idea that I will actually qualify as a lawyer. Now that I am, there is still so much more in my life that I need to explore. I should live my life doing good things to serve others. Greed is a terrible thing- always wanting more and wanting things that other people have. I should aim to serve others and to be a role model for the younger generation. To me, a good life is to always try to do good things. When I feel good, I look good and I am good.

28 January 2019

I travelled to my country of birth again. I am currently at a hotel. It has not been that long since I was last here but unfortunately, my Aunt Tanya passed away on Friday evening and so I booked a flight on Saturday to leave for Sunday. When I visited my Aunt Tanya, not only did I underestimate her illness, I did not realise that was the last time I will see her.

3 February 2019

I am currently in the airport waiting for my flight to return to the UK. This has been a very quick travel and certainly unexpected. My Aunt Tanya unfortunately passed away so I returned to attend her funeral. Aunt Tanya looked after me when I was a child so I treat her like my second mother. I felt I owed to her and to her family that I provide support during this difficult time.

This experience taught me a few things. Firstly, I was able to travel by myself without any issues. Secondly, I discovered a few things about my extended family and the community in my hometown. There were rituals before, during and after the funeral which vary from walking backwards, not leaving the coffin with body alone, washing our hair with chicken blood, not eating noodles and a rather strange way of getting undressed in public and throwing clothes to the river.

Yes – I had to remove my clothes, including my underwear and throw them to the river. I understand we were all grieving, but seriously, I had not taken off my clothes so openly in public like this since maybe I was a kid. I felt embarrassed, confused and dumbfounded to say the least. I could not even express what I really thought as it would be frowned upon if I am not accepting of the rather bizarre tradition so specific to this particular region. I heard other areas had a different tradition which to me seemed like a better option if I were given the choice.

It is difficult to understand the reasons for the rituals but somehow I am caught in it, despite being sceptical about it. Perhaps this is more than just tradition but a way of distraction from the intense grief of bereavement – it is a way for families and the community to unite and support each other by following traditions, as strange as those traditions may be.

9 February 2019

Patrick from ABC asked whether I am still happy to work with them as he will shortly send the contract.

In a weird turn of events, I found out that DE might be offering me a different position from what I initially interviewed for. As I have already accepted ABC's offer, it is all getting a bit complicated.

To add complexity to the mix, one of the girls I trained some time ago and has become my friend, applied for a role that I also applied for. This girl, is called Kim and in fact, I am on my way to see her now. It is going to be a bit odd giving her advice for the position that I applied for. However, I want to remember that there are plenty of jobs out there and that I am not greedy. I can always learn something new. Plus, I am happy with what I have. I have a loving husband, my own home, a promising job offer which is in line with my future goals. I have the potential to do advocacy and develop my skills as a lawyer. The role has a lot of potential and I can always move on to a different firm after I have obtained a few years of PQE. I wish to develop my social skills a bit more and work on relationship building.

18 February 2019

I called in sick today (Monday) as I was not feeling well. I had a cold and my throat felt terrible. The thought of taking instructions in this condition filled me with dread. Staying away from work definitely helped.

26 February 2019

I did not get much sleep yesterday. I only managed to get a few hours of light sleep or maybe even less. Even though I lacked sleep, I was able to function at work. No terrible mistakes as far as I know. I can still supervise the work of others and carry out my own work. I am looking forward to meeting with the Law Commission to simplify the rules.

16 March 2019

I have been offered a job at JK. The firm is in the city dealing with corporate clients. I turned down ABC's job offer. It was very awkward given that we had been negotiating for some time. I was due to start with ABC but then decided to pull out. Patrick, the Partner of ABC interviewed me and he appears to take the rejection personally. It was almost like he purchased a furniture and he was not happy that it was not going to be delivered. Anyway, it is for the best. I have to take my chance in the city and see how it goes.

I can't wait to start working in the city again. I am so looking forward to it. Whatever happens, I have to try.

Today, I woke up at 4:45am. I was able to study from around 5:30am until maybe around 11 am. I studied the guidance. It felt really good being able to study first thing in the morning.

22 March 2019

I put everything on hold to attend a sleep workshop. Is it useful? I am not sure. I supposed I have picked up a few tricks here and there. I like the idea of relaxing and tensing my muscles. I also like the idea of doing something nice after a night of not sleeping well. Only time will tell if my insomnia can get cured.

I am excited to start at my new job at the city. I am really looking forward to it. It will be such a change from my current job. I am going to miss driving to work though. At least I will be able to go to the city every day. I will be able to explore the city a bit more. I will try new restaurants regularly. I will make the most of working in the city. I wonder what the next pages of this journal will bring.

PART 2

Qualified

7. ADMISSION IN LAW, ADMISSION IN LIFE

5 April 2019

It is my admission ceremony today. This ceremony celebrates my admission as a lawyer.

In addition to those who gave me opportunities in the legal field, I owe this achievement to four people in my life.

My grandmother – barely literate and having survived the Japanese invasion, she taught me the value of hard work and instilled in me an inherent belief that I can be what I want to be. When my school friends were playing, she taught me the value of working in the market. When nobody could attend parent meetings when I was in kindergarten, in her care I was able to believe I could make notes from the meeting even though I could not actually read cursive writing at all. I suppose this naivety shielded me from the real world filled with limitations and kept the doors of hope opened.

My Aunt Tanya – she was like my second mother. She encouraged me to attend SPED. Those who obtained high results in the entrance exam can go to school here and fortunately, education was free. From the entrance exam, to finding out whether I was accepted and to getting me ready from 4am to commuting two and half hours with me to get to school each way, she was there throughout the long journey with extraordinary patience. Class Galileo V – at the age of 10, this part of my life made my family view me as and expected me to be an absolute genius when really, I felt like a self-conscious dim wit next to my highly intelligent classmates.

I pretty much did not have a male role model when I was growing up. I always respected Uncle Martin as he was always so responsible to his family and faithful to Aunt Tanya. He was one of the few men I actually looked up to growing up. He taught me how to read. Now that respect is tainted. It just seems that there are very few men in my life that are able to be faithful so this is not helping me build my trust. I am just not sure of what to think of the world anymore.

26 August 2019

It is bank holiday Monday today. Yesterday, a group of us went on a boat and had a BBQ. We played board games and watched a film in an open air cinema. I really enjoy spending time with the closest people to me. It was great fun.

1 September 2019

It is 3:40am on a Sunday. As usual, I can't sleep. Thoughts drifting everywhere.

I remember the passage from Rocky. He said:

"It is not about how hard you hit but how hard you can get hit and keep moving forward, how much you can take and keep moving forward. That is how winning is done. If you know what you are worth, then go out and get what you are worth. But you have to be willing to take the hits and not point fingers saying you are not where you want to be because of him, or her or anybody. Cowards do that and that is not you. You are better than that".

4 September 2019

It is 2:10 in the morning. I realise that I have been qualified as a lawyer for a year. Time has flown by so quickly.

The survey of the house we are buying showed potential asbestos on ceiling. I am not thrilled about this. Not sure if we should proceed with purchasing it. It is something to think about.

5 September 2019

It is 3:40am. Again I have difficulty sleeping. I am drinking night time tea to try help me sleep.

6 September 2019

I woke up but this time it was even earlier that the last few nights. I woke up at midnight so I did not even manage to sleep for a few hours before I embark on this long night of battling to sleep. I cannot even remember since when I have had this insomnia. I think it must have started after my mother passed away. Insomnia replaced my nose bleeds from stress. I guess I was content with replacing nose bleeds with insomnia. No good having nose bleeds so insomnia is lesser of the two evils.

9 September 2019

I realise I still like the area of law I am dealing with. I still feel passionate about it. I have forgotten my passion as my interest was buried in all the headaches I endured in the last few years. Actually, it is what I have always wanted to do and I feel rather lucky that I am in this field that I have always wanted to work in. It I has been a while since I felt this way. I have been complacent, laid back and comfortable. I am ready to feel passion for my field of law again. To be reunited with this passion makes me feel alive. I am ready to tackle my future head on. I love every single corner of this field, whatever section I do. I want the ability to move like a queen in a chess game, but in my current field of law. I want to dedicate my knowledge to this field that I love. I want to learn how to command leadership in this field.

10 September 2019

It is a Tuesday around 11ish in the evening. I was able to get a decent sleep yesterday but following the events today, I can feel a headache towards my right brain.

11 September 2019

It is 2:20am. I am awake again. Well, the decent sleep had a good run whilst it lasted.

14 September 2019

Luke and I went to Hastings for the seafood festival. I had seafood and wine. There was sunshine and the beach. Absolutely loved it. Although our car broke down and we had to be rescued, the day was really good.

22 September 2019

This weekend has been good. I feel more myself. I feel more productive. I was looking into investment and I also did some reading. I cleaned the flat, arranged my wardrobe and drawers. I also had my hair done. I generally feel happier. I want to focus on achieving more things. I am not sure if what I want will happen in the future – if I will be allowed to have a second job with my previous employer. I feel good today and I hope I continue to feel like this throughout the week.

27 September 2019

It is 3:40am on a Friday. Again, I can't sleep.

I am considering options for renewing my practising certificate- whether I should do this myself or if I should renew with a firm. Having a second job working on the weekends will not be easy but we shall see.

I am also considering taking OISC Level 3. I would have to assess it is feasible that I will pass the test. I need to start planning for this.

If I renew my practising certificate with a firm, I will consider taking Solicitor Advocacy next year. Thereafter, I would also have to plan for renewing my Level 2 IAAS accreditation. I have a lot of things that I need to do so I have to focus on this. My husband says I like to torture myself by taking on a lot. He is probably right but I am excited about the future.

28 September 2019

I woke up at 4 something in the morning. It is a Saturday. I consider that sleeping until 4am as a getting a decent night of sleep.

Rather than fighting my insomnia, I decided to do representations instead for the second job where I am a freelancer. By 10 am, I was feeling tired but still could not fall asleep even if I tried.

I was thinking of applying for membership with Women Lawyer's Division. I would have to complete an application form and then be interviewed. It is strange that in order to support women, I have to compete with other women just to get the membership. Does that not defeat the purpose of women being united together? The essence of gender inequality is that the issue is so divided. Women cannot even seem to unite with even just assessing if there are any serious issues remaining or not – so being a member of Women Lawyer's Division should really unite all I would have thought. Anyway in my application, I intend to write that flexible working, including working from home is the future for equality and that government bodies and tribunals should pave the way for encouraging flexible working. The only issue is there would be no incentive to do this unless there is a strong push for it.

29 September 2019

It is a Sunday afternoon. I am listening to an audio book by Warren Buffett. This weekend I have been focusing on investments and learning about them. I hope to continue my learning throughout the next few months.

13 October 2019

We are currently at Odney Club in Berkshire. Luke and his dad are playing poker. I am chilling with Luke's mum having coffee.

8. CALM BEFORE THE STORM

10 November 2019

Has it been nearly a month? I am currently in Doha airport waiting for my connecting flight to go on holiday. I am travelling on my own as Luke could not get days off as this was short notice. There seems to be this stigma about married people travelling by themselves. When I was studying law, I could not find the time to travel. I was also broke as a student and had very little money as a paralegal. I focused on my training contract. Also, my mother was sick. It was one thing after another. Now that I am qualified, I can afford to go on holiday and have accrued annual leave to do so, but there is always a reason not to go on holiday so I thought I should travel in case I don't have the opportunity to do so in the future.

11 November 2019

I have reached my destination. I am in a hotel. I have the TV on running in the background and I am having tea. The hotel is quite nice. It is like an apartment with a living room and a small kitchen. There is also a gym and a pool area. No one else seems to be using the pool so it is great I can have privacy. The restaurant is also nice with breakfast buffet in the morning.

14 November 2019

I travelled to the south where the beach was clear, there were blue waters and white sand. Just had breakfast and sat by the beach. What an amazing view! Apart from the airline losing my luggage, everything else had been great.

18 November 2019

This week has flown by so quickly. I had such a wonderful time. Thankfully, the airline found my luggage and delivered it to me. They also gave me compensation as I had to buy things because I had absolutely nothing with me whilst I was waiting for my luggage. At first I was worried as I did not have anything at all, not even my face wash, make up or clothes. After a while, I became accustomed to not having anything as I only needed my shades and a bikini I bought from a nearby market. That is how I lived until my luggage arrived. When my luggage arrived, I am not sure I really needed my stuff anymore.

The highlight of my holiday is scuba diving. I also enjoyed island hopping, snorkelling and helmet diving. I finally saw white sand and clear blue beaches. I would consider coming back here again. It was a really good holiday. I had finally shut down my brain for a while. The last night I was here, I finally had six hours sleep straight without waking up at all, which I have not had for a long time. I felt free. I could wake up in the middle of the night and can have snacks, not worrying that I am making too much noise. I can have whatever I want to eat, whenever I want to eat it and not worry that others do not want the same thing. I can lay by the beach for hours and not worry that others are bored. My body clock was finally ticking on its own and it relished each moment of freedom.

23 December 2019

Travelled to Italy with Luke. Spending Christmas in Rome, then in Venice. Went sightseeing in Rome, visited museums and lots of churches. I like classical and High Renaissance art so seeing so many museums and architecture was great. We wanted to see the Pope but the queue was long so we decided not to go. Venice was surprisingly expensive. I wanted to ride on a Gondola but thought it was overpriced so went on the waterbus instead. Hotel at Venice had a very rustic feel to it.

26 January 2020

Today we cleared up our documents at home, scanning as much as we can in readiness of our move in March. Hopefully our new house will be ready by then. I can't remember if I mentioned that we are moving to a three bed house. Unfortunately, asbestos was found on the ceiling so we are having this removed. We are also renovating the whole place – new kitchen, bathroom and pretty much every single room of the house. I am very excited but since I have planned everything, it feels like I have already moved in a million times in my head.

I am exactly halfway point in this journal. I wonder how my life will be by the end of this book. What would have changed? Would I still be at my current job JK? What kind of things would I have done to try and contribute towards my goals?

29 January 2020

One of my goals in the long term is to try to become a judge. I want to embody the skills that a judge has in order to make decisions about people and situation. I do not know if I will become a judge but I want to know that I tried my best to embody the skills required to be be one. I have a lot of work ahead of me. Where do I even begin?

Approximately 18 years ago, I had written in my earlier diaries that I wanted to become a lawyer. At that time, I did not think I would actually become one but I expressed it with such passion in writing. In a similar way, my dream of becoming a judge is so far. I have to be so hungry to even reach the vicinity of my next destination.

31 January 2020

It is 1:30am. I have spent about an hour reading. Instead of feeling frustration, I now embrace the hours that I am awake so I am able to spend some time reading and also writing in this journal. I consider that insomnia is now my alone time. I am still able to function during the day so I might as well view this as a gift – a gift of time. I am able to learn more because of this and thus, perhaps I should treasure it rather than think of it so negatively.

I will do whatever it takes to embody the skills required I need. In the next few weeks, I plan to watch Supreme Court cases.

3 February 2020

It is Monday today, around 8:40pm. I worked from home. I have been feeling rather empty for some time. I feel lost; I feel that I serve very minimal purpose, if any.

I long to be a lawyer making a difference in people's lives to the maximum impact and I dream of changing the world.

I am aware that there are so many people that would want the corporate life. My life is very comfortable. Why can't I just be content with a comfortable life? Perhaps I need a sabbatical - maybe for about three months to get my thinking straight again.

On a separate note, I am worried of the recent news of Coronavirus that has predominantly taken over the news in China. It is a deadly virus which can be transmitted from human to human.

4 February 2020

It is a Tuesday, 9:05pm. I am having camomile tea as I hope this would allow me to sleep throughout the night.

Work today was busy as usual. People chasing me here, there and everywhere. I want to start saying no to new work but then at the same time, I do not want to run out of work and not bill anything.

I have come to realise that although I want an opportunity, it does not necessarily mean that I will get it. I have to work towards it. I have to give it my best. Some people maybe naturally talented – but I have to work harder than most people to even get half as close to where others are. I have come to accept this in reality. When I was looking for a training contract, I remember being prepared to apply to as many firms as possible and write however many journals in order to accomplish this goal. I was prepared to do whatever it took. For some strange reason, I am finding my next few goals a lot more difficult – or have I just forgotten how hard it truly is to work towards dreams?

On a separate note, I had a pretty decent sleep last night. I felt refreshed in the morning. I normally have a permanent headache throughout the day but today, my head was clear. I hope I am able to sleep through tonight again.

5 February 2020

I was so stressed today at work and I am not even sure why. I feel that I brought the stress to myself and I don't want it to get to me. I have a headache when I left work but it is now better. I can really do with a sabbatical at some point. I would like to live my life stress free, even if it is just for three months. Am I afraid to truly enjoy or appreciate my life as perhaps I fear losing what I have?

Sometimes I am worried - just worried about things. I guess that is part of what I do. I get paid to deal with client's problems so I am having to take on their constant worry. Perhaps I would bene-fit from counselling. I will speak to my friend, Annie- she men-tioned she may have a few contacts that could help me out.

Perhaps I need something to look forward to. I was looking for-ward to buying a house but now that we have bought it and I have planned it all to my heart's content, it feels like I have lived in the house for years already even though we have not even moved in yet. It is almost like when I plan, I get excited but once I have planned it and there are only easy steps left to take as I know it is going the way I planned, I feel like I want another project. Why?

I seem to not appreciate what I have and I can't bring myself to enjoy my comfortable life. There always seems to be a problem and it is hard to relax. I always seem to want to think outside the box but still forgetting I need to maintain what is inside the box.

9 February 2020

It is a Sunday afternoon. Yesterday, I worked for five hours free-lancing in my second job. I prepared witness statements and read materials regarding an appeal. This means that today feels like a Saturday. Thank goodness I have tomorrow as a day off.

Today, I have been super lazy. I spent the majority of my morning in bed. I might work out soon.

10 February 2020

My laziness has reached its absolute peak. I was supposed to give Luke a lift to work. I did not even do that. I guess I feel guilty as I always seem to be on the go. The problem is that when I am supposed to do mundane things that I know needs to be done, I cannot bring myself to do them.

3:10pm

I have tidied up, worked out, showered but not done what I am supposed to. I pretty much relaxed. I should not feel guilty that I have been lazy. If I could have a "Ground Hog Day" it would be days like this. I think this is good for my mental health.

15 February 2020

It is a Saturday morning. I absolutely love that we have already cleaned our place and we are now relaxing. Yesterday, my previous boss had a party to celebrate his 25th wedding anniversary. It made me think how warm and welcoming his guests were. I also did not realise that my previous boss contributes towards helping the homeless.

It is my day off on Monday and I am working from home on Tuesday. Having days off feel great. I can relax and I have time to contemplate life.

By the way, yesterday I encountered a racist taxi driver. He made comments about people from my country of birth. I don't want to dwell on it too much as it is simply a waste of energy. It made me think that if a person is a bigot, that is their problem – unless he is preaching to the whole nation trying to convince others of what he believes in, I hardly think I can convince this guy's permanent views to change in a matter of seconds – certainly not long enough for me to pay any more than I have to towards the meter in the taxi. The way that I see it, my husband awaits at home for me and he is more than happy for me to remain in the UK where I belong and that is more important. I think that perhaps in some way, I have matured and exhausted the frustration revolving the race argument. I now try to choose my battles carefully so I save my energy in order to win those that truly count. Increasing minority in the workforce – yes this is important, argument with driver that I will never see again – absolutely pointless.

16 February 2020

Luke and I had a really great time yesterday. We had dinner and watched a comedy act. It was great fun, I think it helped that I was not working on Saturday. Although I was not able to be productive, I managed to create a website. It is coming along nicely. The purpose of this website is to inspire others to achieve their goals in life.

I met up with a friend, Jonas today. We had a good catch up. This break has helped me to relax and I am starting to feel happier which is the first in a long time.

This week, I want to focus on my well-being. I am going to be working on Saturdays again with my freelance work. Perhaps I should do early hours, from 8am to 1pm so I can have the rest of the day to do what I want. Somehow, I stopped kickboxing as it always seem to be closed when I am not working. I do hope I can make time for kickboxing as I really enjoyed this.

17 February 2020

I had a relaxing day today as it was my day off, in addition to the full weekend I had. It really shows just how much being stressed out at work can do. I have always been able to handle stress but having time off really highlights that just because I can handle stress, it does not mean I should expose myself to so much of it.

18 February 2020

It is the second week that I have taken Monday off as annual leave. Although work is relatively easy, there are a few cases that I worry about.

19 February 2020

I was able to follow a routine today which is great. I managed to do quite a bit of work in the morning and I was able to leave on time. I went kickboxing which also felt great. When I reached home, I still had the energy to tidy up and do the dishes. I also had time to pamper myself with face mask.

This morning, I tried to visualise what it would be like when I am 50 years old. Hopefully, I would be able to retire early by then.

20 February 2020

It is Thursday night. I made an effort this week to finish on time or leave earlier than usual from work as I normally work until quite late. I am still stressed out but I am able to cope with it better when I leave on time. I am also able to work to go kickboxing which also helps my stress level. I am able to channel my frustration physically.

Luke's eye is sore. I am worried about him. I hope he will be ok.

Time has flown by quickly. I have been at JK for about ten months.

21 February 2020

Today, my colleague Joseph criticised the efforts of trying to get BAME into particular workforce. He effectively said that BAME should not get a privileged platform for diversity purposes. Not only did he say this, he was encouraging others to agree with him. I could not believe my ears. He wants to reverse the longstanding efforts carried out in the last decades for equality purposes. Not only is he saying this, but the sticking point is that he is actually managing to convince others, spreading it like an infectious disease. I was stunned. I want to pick my battles when it comes to race but is this one of them? I was worried that if I speak out that people might not like me and I might lose my job. But what kind of a job is worth working for if I can't even stand up to the principles set out for equality purposes? What is the purpose of my practising certificate qualifying me as a lawyer, having practised in human rights if it is not for such situations?

If I defend this race argument and I end up losing my job or I am somehow victimised because of it, then so be it. In a few seconds, I assessed what grounds it could fall under in employment law discrimination claim and although I have not done employment law since law school, I had a feeling I stood a chance.

I spoke out. Yes, I voiced my disagreement indirectly - somehow, the words flowed out so naturally without even a mere hesitation. It was almost like I rehearsed it as it felt relatively easy to tackle this argument. I suppose all of those years from when I was 13 years old writing in my diary about equality and eventually studying human rights law were the rehearsals for such a moment.

23 February 2020

I want to learn a bit of everything but at the same time, I want to relax and have a great life. Perhaps I should change fields, but I know of no other area of law. Perhaps I should work in equality cases. But we seem to have reached a relatively secure stage in equality law. We cannot eliminate all forms of discrimination, but the legal tools are there to argue and defend should it be necessary.

I thought I knew what I want. Now I am questioning whether I only sought the title of being a lawyer. I would not like think that it is just for the title. I have contemplated deeply about simply taking a step back and enjoying my life. In fact, in the last few weeks of taking Mondays off have been really helpful in my mental well-being.

24 February 2020

It is a Monday night I had my third annual leave on a Monday. There is something about having a day off on a Monday that makes the world feel slower. The kickboxing facility s empty for instance. There are less people in public transport and shopping centre. Overall there is a more peaceful feeling.

What would my ideal life look like – relaxing life, fulfilling job and decent pay. It is a lot to ask for I suppose. I do not even have any children yet I am creating so much drama in my life.

25 February 2020

Today, I sat in a telephone conference – pretty much just listened in. At this point, I wondered how much legal knowledge really came into use. Securing the client was more about tactic and making connections rather than law. It is really more about busines or commercial awareness.

This evening, I watched Judge Judy. I watched her ask a series of fact finding questions very similar to how I questioned clients before when taking instructions for witness statements. Judge Judy's mind is very sharp. I remember when I used to prepare witness statements, I had a clear image of what was being described and any deviation from it stood out - that's what the mind notices and that is why it appears sharp.

I guess I want a bit of both worlds – the skill to navigate in business but the sharpness of a litigation lawyer.

Perhaps the problem is that I have never had anything so good for a long enough period of time that even if I had the best thing in front of me, either I cannot tell or I do not attach myself to it in case I lose it. Perhaps in a twisted and ironic way, I not only lack trust in people but also the world in general. Maybe deep down, it is hard for me to trust the world. Perhaps deep down, I am preparing myself in case things go wrong as a way to protect myself like I have always done when I was younger because it was necessary to get by.

Moving forward, I have to trust in myself. I can handle the majority of things that come my way. I also have to trust in other people. Not every single person has intentions like my father. The majority of people generally behave in an acceptable way. I have to trust that others are willing and are accepting of most people and the majority have a good side to them that they want to share. Lastly, I must learn to trust the world. The world has sheltered and so far continued to house my life. Although I am a miniscule part of this big world, I must accept that the world is generally a positive place that can allow me to get by with some level of happiness.

27 February 2020

Two support staff members are leaving. One is going to FC, my previous employer – the firm that made all support staff redundant. Makes me realise that there is so much excitement around FC but I feel it is slightly overrated.

8 March 2020

I am quite excited about tomorrow. I am attending a court hearing for my freelance work. Counsel will be there. I hope it all goes well and that I can observe the hearing with relative straightforwardness.

10 March 2020

Yesterday, I attended the hearing. Actually I attended two hearings. I enjoyed the first one which was granted on the spot. Client was so happy he kissed counsel. In the second hearing, it was a bit more complicated. Observing hearings is definitely a learning curve, not just in terms of the legal and practical aspects but also the human side of it – that each case is important, embroiled with client emotions.

9. MOVING FORWARD

16 March 2020

I am starting to become concerned about Coronavirus. There is a growing number of deaths and of infected people in the UK. This virus has already infected and caused a lot of deaths in Europe, China and other countries. I am concerned that the UK is slow in implementing action and is prioritising the economy to the detriment and risk to people's lives. Because of this concern, honestly I do not feel motivated to go into the office. I feel that I want to take matters in my own hands and just wait it out until the government figures out the issue and provide clear guidance to tackle this problem. Businesses are being led by the government and as it stands, we have no clear guidance. There is a part of me that feels businesses should take initiative to issue guidance to employees despite lacking clear instructions from the government. As it remains to be business as usual, I am particularly concerned about the next few weeks. There is a part of me that wants to take sabbatical so I do not have to physically go to the office and resume working once this virus is over. How can I care about someone's case when I can see the world is falling apart? We are only a few weeks away from reaching the state of Italy's pandemic situation.

I hope that the government issues guidance for people to either work from home, to close or go in lockdown and for everyone to wear protective clothing. Everything is still continuing as normal and I am concerned that my loved ones who are obliged to continue going to the office because the government is leading them this way.

I wonder what the next few weeks will bring. I want to know what Boris Johnson will say this afternoon in his speech. I want to just sleep it all off and pretend it is not happening.

I want to make an impact. I want to be remembered for something larger than myself. Perhaps that is why I do not feel fulfilled. I think maybe I just want a short break with a period of nothingness, maybe two to three months break would be good for me. I am tired of chasing money, promotion or achievements. I want to live my life and be present in what I am doing, even for only two to three months.

18 March 2020

I have been feeling down today.

Do I even know myself? Sure, I am a lawyer. I come from a fairly humble background. I am quiet, passionate and ambitious. I can be fiery, overcomplicated and yet be cold. I like being quiet – can't go wrong with not saying much. I don't like showing my vulnerable side or any weak points. Perhaps I am vain; some may say narcissistic. I am human. I worry a lot about the present and the future. I hang on to things that I should let go from the past.

Time goes by so quickly. Years that have gone by seems like just months. It will be four years this coming October since my mother passed away but the events are still quite vivid in my memory. If only I can have selective memory. Recently, I feel like I am drowning – in work, relationships and in life. I know there are a lot of things I should be grateful for but I take these for granted. Maybe I am not so good in slowing down. Maybe I am just better equipped at working 24/7. Perhaps I am just more resilient that way as there is less time for worry and negative thinking.

10:13pm

My work has announced we can work from home full time due to the virus. Hopefully, this would be less risk for us in catching the virus although I will miss going outside.

It is odd to understand that when I started this journal, there was no way I could envisage some of the events occurring in today's news – for instance, the Coronavirus which started in China and has spread to the rest of the world including the UK. This virus, otherwise known as Covid19 is contagious. The virus attacks the lungs, can cause pneumonia and for those with underlying illnesses, it could result to death. This pandemic has already take so many people's lives. It has reached the UK and of course, there is worry that loved ones could catch it.

19 March 2020

It feels like the world has gone mad. There are now 144 deaths in the UK due to Covid19 and about 2,000 people are infected. There are over 3,000 people dead in Italy and a similar amount in China.

I worry that Luke would have to keep going to work as the courts remain open. I have written to The Law Society in the hope they can influence the courts. I have also started a petition to have lockdown with other countries. So far, there has been no response. Action in the UK seems rather slow in comparison to China, a country that can build a hospital in 10 days. It is becoming difficult to get food in the supermarket as everyone seems to be panic buying. We have had to get as much as we can as the shelves in the supermarket are empty. It is also becoming difficult to order online. There are still available delivery slots but who knows if we will actually receive the delivery. Right now, Luke is at a supermarket – it is almost 10 pm. He thinks that the supermarket will deliver fresh items around this time of the week. He thinks he can get items before the crowd gets there on Friday.

I worry about the future. I hope it will be fine – but the question is when? I think the government's actions should be more pre-emptive and stronger when it comes to the virus. The government seems to throw money at the problem to support businesses. However, it is worrying that health care workers do not have sufficient PPE required.

21 March 2020

The government has finally asked restaurants to close in order to prevent further spread of the virus.

23 March 2020

I finally received confirmation that my petition has been author-ised. Now there is a more difficult task of getting signatures for it. Some people that I know are good and are likely to sign, but others are probably not going to sign it. However, for me it is more about creating awareness so as long as it does that then I am happy.

4 April 2020

We are reaching 3,600 deaths due to Covid 19 in the UK. It feels like we are waiting for a storm to come.

I have been furloughed which means that I get to stay home not working and have 80% of my salary paid. Although these are difficult times, I can't help but feel lucky as I have been wanting a break. This is probably the only silver lining in this whole situation.

I will try to use this time off from next week until 31 May 2020 to be productive. I intend to learn more about advocacy and Higher Rights.

It is weird that I have been wanting a break - it is almost like God heard my prayers. Unfortunate for others who are affected by the pandemic though.

6 April 2020

It is 5:50am and I cannot sleep any longer. I have a day filled with trying to do handover and finishing off as much work as I can.

I don't know where to begin when talking about what is going in the world. I guess to summarise the situation in the UK, we are all waiting for the worst to come. I am hopeful that once the worst has come, everything will settle down, the vaccine will be devel-oped and distributed so everything can go back to normal.

During these difficult times, I want to count my blessings. So far, no one that I know has been affected of Covid19 even though I have a lot of family who are health care workers. Working in a city firm means that there is more flexibility in working from home during this pandemic. I was able to go on a few holidays just before the outbreak of the virus. Now I am able to stay home with 80% salary paid. I consider that I am very lucky indeed. I am surprised how unscathed I have been in this tragedy. I have never felt so lucky in my entire life.

12 April 2020

It is Easter Sunday. We continue to be on lockdown. It is weird that I could not go to church today. I watched the mass online of the Pope in an empty church.

13 April 2020

Today is Easter Monday. I never had a bike as a kid so never learnt how to ride one– presumably I was never given one as bikes were too expensive. Luckily, our new house came with a used bike just my size. It was the perfect opportunity to learn how to ride a bike during this furlough. After two sessions of me yelling at Luke not to let go when pushing the bike, I am glad to say I now managed to learn how to ride a bike! More importantly, I have not fallen from the bike as yet so I am very happy about that!

2 May 2020

Good news – my furlough has been extended until 30 June. I was prepared to go for unpaid leave to take sabbatical. Although it would have been nice to travel or move into our new house. However, we are on lockdown and so nobody can go anywhere. Nevertheless, I am still enjoying every minute of this furlough. I can't believe the world is on my side during this pandemic. Thankfully every person that I am close to are ok during this pandemic.

14 May 2020

I had a nose bleed thinking about how much I hated my father. I don't want to go over the thoughts again. Am I really going to be upset about this whole thing that it can cause me to have nose-bleeds? I don't want to waste any more energy on him. I need to find a silver lining in what happened.

26 May 2020

Yesterday, I thought about why my father's actions still affect me today. I realise that my father being absent in my life and the events that occurred before, helped put me in a position where I can learn a strong work ethic. I endured hardship because of what my father did. Due to this hardship as a child, I was more driven to become successful and resilient. Naïve as it may sound, I feel that hardship fuelled my ambitions and with this ambition, I can do something meaningful in my life. I can use the hardship I experienced to motivate me to reach my next goals in life.

On a separate note, I saw an article from a member of Women's Lawyer Division expressing their views that working from home could benefit female lawyers. Flashback to my application to the Women's Lawyer Division where I explained this exact argument about equality. It is great to see that someone has read my thoughts and agree with them.

28 May 2020

I have been contemplating about my life. The puzzle I have been trying to solve all my life – I have finally understood it. With this newly defined purpose, I hope to contribute to those that are greatly impacted in the society. I hope to focus my energy within this narrow purpose and not be distracted by immaterial things. I have a fairly clear vision of what I want and I am ready to give myself to it. I will give it the best possible chance of success. I am ready. This furlough has allowed me time to contemplate and I now feel mentally strong. I am ready to give myself whole-heartedly in order to contribute to meaningful purpose.

I would need to embody the character of a lawyer in pursuit of a well-meaning goal. The goal to help others by being genuine and minimise any self-interest. I must learn to be less vain; to have more empathy towards others; go back to basics and learn the meaning of justice. I have the ability (and qualifications) to truly make an impact in this world yet somehow, I am restricting myself from doing so. I affirm to myself that I intend to pursue justice wherever possible. I am a tool for the legal profession; I will use my legal skills as a sword if required or calm a storm if need be. I am blessed to be a lawyer and I owe it to myself, the legal profession and the world to use my skills in the most honourable way. I am a lawyer beyond a rubber stamp. I am a lawyer with a responsibility towards the next generation to carry out justice in law.

2 June 2020

Today, I listened and read a case assessing if a vase is part of a building or not. I listened to the recorded hearing on the Supreme Court website. I also read the judgment. It is interesting to listen to the arguments put forward by the QC. I wish to adopt the mannerisms the advocates use in court. I wish to imitate their capabilities and skills in addressing complex questions put forward by the judges. I also wish to learn more about the judges themselves – their background and how they managed to reach the position they are in. Whether or not my goals transpire, I hope my career will at least follow an interesting trajectory.

15 June 2020

We have now moved into our new house. We moved when the carpet was still not fitted. The place was nearly done but needed a lot of cleaning due to the renovation. Anyway, I am very pleased as to how the house has turned out. The kitchen is brand new. We have a dishwasher as well. Although there was a mistake with the carpet, I quite like how it has turned out. I love the sofa – it is light blue with storage and is a corner sofa. It also converts to a bed. I am also pleased that the bathroom is new. We have a bath with toilet upstairs and a second toilet downstairs. We have three bedrooms with the smallest room turned into an office.

Tomorrow, I will be returning to our flat to paint the walls . We are hoping to sell our flat or have it rented out.

29 June 2020

I am so happy with my life. I have never lived in such luxury and have never had it so good.

30 June 2020

I have a meeting with my employer at 4pm. It is a business update hosted by the Director. I feel that it would either be good or bad news. Either way, I am bracing myself for it. I don't want to worry as yet but I am curious. It is so sudden. It could either be redundancy or working from home permanently. I wonder what I will be writing later on.

5 July 2020

It is 11pm on a Saturday. Still on furlough. It turned out that my employer intends to make 13 people redundant. We shall find out in the next few weeks who will be made redundant. I am not sure how to feel about the whole thing. I have to remain positive about it. We don't know who will be made redundant as yet. Best to start looking for a new job just in case.

I am thinking of applying to be a lawyer for the government. The more I take it seriously, the more I feel anxious about the process. I should just start the application. If get the job then that's great. If not, I am already living a comfortable life. I just know that not trying in this current climate is not an option.

In the past few years, my life has been going brilliantly. I guess there is a worry that these good things could come to an end.

I have just started my application as a lawyer for the government. I can't help but feel anxious about the whole thing. I am not sure if other people feel the same was I do about these things.

I suppose all I can do is try my best. If I do not get accepted, then it is not the end of the world. Then perhaps it was not meant to be, but I would like this opportunity to be for me. I would like to believe that I am destined to do something that can make an impact in the society. Although I know that not every single opportunity is for me, I want to think that I have qualified as a lawyer because I am destined to use it for a good purpose.

Who knows what I will end up writing on the application? Who knows what will happen with the application? I have no idea. All I can do is try.

I have everything I could need, want and more. Yet trying to apply for a new job is somehow making me anxious. Perhaps I should just enjoy the feeling of want. Perhaps being content is just something that I am not accustomed to.

I applied for the position. I certainly did not rush the application but I also did not spend a lifetime completing it. I do not know if I will get through the next stage. There are a quite a few stages. I am starting to feel passionate about this role.

I remember being made redundant just under five years ago. I remember being really surprised and upset then. Now I guess I am pretty used to how it works. The passion I had for this field is now starting to wear off. I remember in my journal – I said I wanted to know everything about this field – that was five years ago. How things change. Now I want to know other areas of law and work for the public service.

8 July 2020

It looks like I am due to finish this journal very soon. A lot sooner than expected. I wanted to know the result of the job application before I start the next journal. It is all part of the journey so whether it is good news or bad news, I have to be prepared to record it, learn from it, improve my skills and move on to the next step.

I can't believe I am on my last page of this journal. This journal has captured some of the most exciting moments in my life. It has captured my qualifying as a lawyer, getting married, travelling on my own, finding a new job and buying a house. I am now going to start a new journal.

PART 3

Renewed Purpose

10. DREAMING

9 July 2020

I write this new journal at a position of being at risk to possible redundancy. I am yet to find out next week if I am going to be made redundant. I am lucky that I have freelance work that I can ask for more hours if that is the case.

In the meantime, I have applied as a lawyer for the government. I am due to complete the critical thinking assessment next week. Let's just say that doing such tests do not come naturally to me. I have to have some understanding of what this test would entail. I honestly do not know if I will pass the test or if I will get through the next few stages. The concept of a job offer for this position seems so exciting yet almost miraculous. At least I am able to learn a bit about critical thinking tests which would help me in my day to day job anyway. Whatever happens, I would have to record it and deal with whatever comes my way.

10 July 2020

I studied and practiced questions in preparation for the critical thinking test next week. When I thought of preparing for the test a few days ago, somehow I envisaged that I will improve my skills almost instantly. In reality, preparing for the test went from bad to even more complicated. By the afternoon, I started to feel deflated and my confidence was low. My scores were rather average or if not, then likely to be below average. It did not look like my new results were any better than the initial ones. I was nowhere near where I wanted to be in terms of scores, it truly felt like I have a long road ahead of me. I was also unsure if the correct answers that I managed to get were scored by luck or if I actually understood the question and answered correctly. I was also concerned that it does not seem remotely possible that I could get through the end stage of job offer as it seems difficult to get through the next stage. It also seemed like I am studying principles, but I am simply unable to apply it during the test under time constraints.

Thankfully, I managed to score 14 correct answers out of 15 for one section. This is the highest score I have had so far. Although the result is not necessarily reflective of my overall progress and current skill level, it gave me the much needed hope to boost my confidence that even though getting through this test would be very difficult, there is a possibility that I would go through. I have to hang on to the small possibility and continue to persevere in the next few days. It is not ideal to be preparing during the weekend, especially since Luke is unaware that I applied for this position. I chose not to tell him because it would put a lot of pressure on me as I would care a lot about what he thinks. It may also distract me as I am more likely to be anxious if I knew people are aware, in case I am rejected. I think it is best if I try to get through the next stage on my own without anyone knowing. It will take a lot of determination to focus and persevere in my preparation for the test given Luke will likely want to spend time together or he would expect that I am available generally. I think I will call it a night, get some sleep and start early tomorrow. I could study all night tomorrow if I do not feel that my skills have significantly improved or if I feel that my progress is inconsistent.

13 July 2020

It is 12:45am. I have yet to sleep. I have been studying and practising the critical thinking test that I am due to take this day or tomorrow. Quite frankly, I am getting tired of studying this test. I am also not sure how it is possible for me to get lower scores the more I practice. Perhaps I should just take the test so I can move on with my life. I am starting to feel like this test has taken over my life. At this stage, I am honestly unsure as to whether I will pass through the next stage. Whatever happens, I have got to proceed with the test. I am certain that not going for it will not be an option. That would be more of a failure than a rejection. I will always look back wondering "what if".

I am also due to find out whether my position with my current employer is at risk of redundancy. Today might be an eventful day. Perhaps that is why I do not want to sleep. I shall do something nice to treat myself whatever happens.

10:52am

I practiced another critical thinking test. My result was unfortunately worse than I expected. I am in a reasonable frame of mind yet I appear to be overthinking the answers. I feel helpless as the answers are so definitive. In real life, I can attempt to argue in various ways. Although the final product may not be perfect, it would be sufficient to submit and move the issue forward. Also, I expected that I would progress at a steep curve showing successful results in a matter of days. Unfortunately, that is not the case.

I did the critical thinking test this afternoon as I wanted to get it over and done with. I could no longer stand practicing for and it felt the more I practiced, the further my results became lower. Anyway, I ran out of time because I inadvertently completed the example questions. There is nothing more I can do. I am just glad it is done.

On a different note, I have not had any email from my current employer so I am guessing I have not been made redundant. I am so relieved that I can finally just do other things and relax. I will try enjoy this evening.

16 July 2020

I am grateful that I have not been selected for redundancy. Not only that, my furlough leave has also been extended until 31 August 2020. This would bring my furlough leave up to nearly five months which is great as I really enjoyed my furlough leave.

21 July 2020

Perhaps I am delusional. Delusional in believing I could work as a lawyer for the government and for me to reach my goals. I am so far from the truth and reality.

When I was a paralegal, I thought that all I needed to do is find a training contract, which at that time I considered as the holy grail of the legal profession. When I qualified as a lawyer, I thought that it would all suddenly become easier and that jobs would line up for me or I would be headhunted. I thought I would have a different command in my career and have a different kind of authority. I thought that once I qualified as a lawyer, I would change the world. How wrong was I? How very wrong indeed.

I am of course grateful that I was better paid than before and I do have a comfortable life. In that sense, I am very lucky. I have a husband who loves me. To many, I have done well, including my friends.

Perhaps I am too hard on myself. I am not sure what I expected. I am not sure why I am impatient. I guess I am freaking out about not being any closer to my goals.

27 July 2020

I had forgotten I sent my CV to DZ along with applying for the government lawyer role. This is the only other role I had applied to as it advertised case work in Judicial Review cases. I had been so caught up with the other one that I had forgotten about DZ. Anyway, they would like to have an interview this Wednesday. I will prepare tomorrow. I am still not sure whether I will really leave my current job as I have not been made redundant. However, given that the interview has already been set then I might as well just go ahead with it.

29 July 2020

Furlough unexpectedly ending today. Back to work tomorrow. Still get to work from home.

I had an interview today with DZ. I think it went well although slightly concerned the role might not actually have Judicial Review unless one of my cases reach that point. Defeats the purpose as I will try my best not to reach Judicial Review if starting from bottom applications so I might never get any Judicial Review.

2 August 2020

I had a bad dream about my government lawyer interview. Although I have not received any confirmation of an interview for this position, I had a dream that I was wearing trainers and shorts. I only realised this when I was at the interview and I left before I could be asked to go in. I left to look for proper attire but the queue to purchase the shoes were so long I ended up missing the interview. Thank goodness it was just a dream.

4 August 2020

I received a job offer from DZ but I politely declined. Although DZ is a reputable firm, I don't think it is the firm is for me. The role will also involve starting the applications from beginning so it is pretty much like any other role. I would just be moving from one firm to another doing similar applications and I do not see any point in that.

6 August 2020

Although today was a very busy and challenging day, the day turned around for me when I received an email regarding the government lawyer position. Unbelievably, I was through the next stage. It feels really amazing to be able to get through. I feel that it is an achievement even to reach this stage. I am celebrating inside and I will treasure this feeling for as long as possible.

8 August 2020

The prospect of interview is making my dream become so real in my imagination. I wonder what the technical legal exercise entails. I suspect it might be the changes the government is thinking about relating to limiting the scope of Judicial Review for judges. Alternatively, it could be about Brexit issues. Whatever happens, I have to give it my best shot. This is it. This is a once in a lifetime opportunity. I can always apply next year of course but I feel that this year, I am ready.

I remember wanting to apply for the government lawyer role when I was in university, only to realise that I could only apply once I am about to qualify as a lawyer. With the pursuit to qualify, I guess I had put this route to one side.

10 August 2020

How is my work at my job getting busier by the day?

How am I also able to write so much in what seems like a short period of time?

Although I would like to work out regularly, I seem to be working later and later by the day. The amount of emails coming seems crazy. Working in the city in the 21st century means that every client wants an immediate response all the time and all clients respond to emails even quicker.

11 August 2020

I don't know why but I am staying later and later by the day. I realise that my insomnia is probably linked to feeling stressed at work. My insomnia has started again. I am waking up at around 3am.

12 August 2020

Today, I spoke to clients and tried to help each individual. Helping the clients were somewhat more enjoyable today. I don't aim to please but I try to get to the bottom of what it is they are looking for and see what the position is in practice. From now on, I will intentionally set out to help people. Also, I found that providing comfort is half the job. Comfort in advising but also realistic and managing expectation. I must remember to help each individual - to understand what it is they want and then make a connection that way, as well as alleviating their concerns.

26 August 2020

Time for work again. Laptop slow to load again. I am truly hopeful that I can finish work on time today. I say this every day and I have not managed to do it yet but I really think that I can finish work on time today.

In the last few evenings after work, I was reading about Boris Johnson, the prorogation and the reasons why it was done.

Today, I was able to finish work before 7pm so getting closer to my goal of finishing at 5:30pm. I feel good today and don't feel as tired.

27 August 2020

Work again. I really feel that this day is the day I will finish on time. I am optimistic about this day. I think maybe the best way to finish on time is to book something just after work. Maybe tomorrow I will book a massage after work.

6 September 2020

It is Sunday. I am pretty content with my life.

I looked at the competency criteria for the interview. There were only three so I should be able to prepare for it and finish it quickly. If this was grounds of appeal, I would have completed this by now as there would be a deadline.

I am eager to work for the government as a lawyer and also to become a civil servant. This means that even in my personal life, I have to make sure I hold integrity. I would carry not just my own, family and legal profession's reputation but also the government's reputation on behalf of the country.

I want to develop my character. I have been a lawyer for some time and I have to start owning this role. Why don't I feel like I own this role? Am I truly going to feel like a lawyer again anytime soon. Is that why I want to work as a government lawyer – so I can humour myself and feel like an actual lawyer? Perhaps I am too harsh on myself. Is manifesting my goal really more about transforming into someone I am not because I was never fulfilled as a child? Is my search for transformation because I want to hide what was missing in my past? Is this dream really more about trying to figure myself out? I hope I can find my feet in navigating through something meaningful in life.

9 September 2020

I so want my current job to be the job I feel truly passionate about. However, I am not feeling that way. It is stressful yet comfortable. It is a never ending conveyer belt of corporate work and emails. In the corporate sector, structure and speedy responses are welcomed; creativity is rare, if somewhat lost.

I am currently listening to Debussy, Claire de Lune. This is the song that I heard and have since searched for the title. I had to scour through various classical music to find this. It is such a beautiful song.

It is 8:15pm. I received the email for the government lawyer position requesting completion of the technical assessment. I am so looking forward to this because I want to get the ball rolling. I will do this on the weekend.

12 September 2020

I need to establish what it is I need to do to be able to prepare for the technical assessment. I suppose I should be able to draft policies at a minimum. I know that it will be about public law but would it relate to issues such as Prorogation? I guess I better prepare for the worst. I will prepare until 12pm.

13 September 2020

I am about to take the technical assessment. I am not sure how to feel. Whatever happens, I will be kind to myself.

11pm

I took the technical assessment today. I was able to write a response which is something.

14 September 2020

It is 10pm. In the last few days, I was thinking about my father. I realise that he was a sociopath. This is much more digestible in my brain than thinking of my father as a criminal. This way, I can explain to myself that he was a sick man rather than an evil one.

Perhaps I should get in touch with my paternal aunts as I do not really know them.

16 September 2020

It turns out that I will be returning to furlough which is great. I can't wait. This is exactly what I need. That has made my day. I can't want to go back on furlough.

17 September 2020

I just read an article and it explores the concept of making stress my friend, to make it work for me. I guess that is what I am doing already. I don't want fear and anxiety to be part of my assessment in problem solving. In a job where I am paid to worry about other people's problems, how do I carry out the work without worrying?

Do I simply shrug my shoulders and just carry on with the job? Do I reassure myself into believing I have back up plans and emergency solutions? How do I assess my problems or any potential problems without feeling fear or anxiety? Do I need a distraction whilst I am doing the task that makes me feel anxious? Do I feel anxious about problem solving or is it that I care? Does caring a lot about something result in fear or anxiety? Does uncertainty trigger anxiety?

I have realised that I am halfway through this journal and what a topic to be discussing at the midway point. Ironic that anxiety is at the centre of my mind and is also at the centre of this journal.

Is it the feeling that I need to feel something? If I do not feel sleepy, tired, happy then I feel anxious. Is it that I have pretty much had my whole life surrounded by drama that when I do not have it, my life feels mundane? Do I replace the feeling of nothingness with fear because feeling something is what I have always felt and known? How do I move forward to problem solving without feeling anything about problem solving? How I do I attach positive emotions to my day to day living?

21 September 2020

My first day back on furlough and an hour into it, I get called back to work This is a devastating blow as I had hoped to get some time to prepare for the interview. Now the pressure is really on to deliver.

22 September 2020

I woke up around 5ish in the morning and started preparing for the interview from 6:30am. I started work from 9am. I am feeling dazed.

25 September 2020

It is 8:20am. I was thinking yesterday that I have a lot of good things in my life so whatever happens with the interview, I cannot be too devastated. I have no reason to feel any anxiety. I think the reason why I feel this is perhaps because I have hardly had stability in life before this. This is the first time that I have ever felt stable for this long so even when my circumstances are stable, I cannot truly feel it. I always have an expectation that my world could crumble at any point, like it has always done when I was a child, being separated from my father, leaving my grandmother, moving to another country and so on. My early formative years consisted of so many changes at least every five years or so that the only thing consistent was that things will change. I have to expect changes in my life and that is why it is harder for me to feel secure. I need a strong mechanism to handle things when or if it is going wrong.

I think that in the eyes of my brother and cousin, it looks like I have made it – to them, it was slightly inevitable. In the eyes of my friends, it looks like I have done well in life unexpectedly. In my husband's eyes, I am an ambitious genius albeit slightly lacking common sense. In the eyes of the legal profession, I comply with the rules and as far as they are concerned, I am an average lawyer. In the eyes of my colleagues, I am generally an introvert, slightly detached and somewhat strange – unique but rather strange. I am probably all of those things, but more so in different circumstances with different people. In the instability of my early formative years, I have become adaptable. That is how I have come to know how to get to the next step. When there are policy changes, I am cautious but I try to get it right – not perfect, but just that bit more attempt to be adept because my whole life since a child has continuously changed. Fortunately or unfortunately, perhaps my default settings are programmed to naturally thrive in instability albeit with constant and sometimes unnecessary cautiousness.

11. THE INTERVIEW

26 September 2020

It is a Saturday night, 11:20pm. My interview is on Monday. I would have like to be prepared for the interview by today but looks like I might have to prepare tomorrow. At least I was able to get Monday off.

Perhaps there really is no right or wrong answer for the most part but simply how I come across. I expect that I would be nervous. Although I want this job, I have to see things in a bigger perspective. Yes, I have been working hard for this role but if it does not work out, it is not the end of the world. Really. Life will still go on. I will still go on. It is good to be driven and to get to the goal as close as possible. It is even better if I do get there. But if not, it is fine. There is no need to feel down about it. I will simply have to take a different route in my journey.

I think I have to look at this in this perspective. They need to hire someone and they are looking for people who will not step out of line and who will follow protocols. They are not necessarily looking for someone who is a genius but rather a candidate who is capable – a highly capable individual.

27 September 2020

It is Sunday, 10:45pm. It is the night before the interview. I have tried to prepare as much as I can today. I am feeling fine at the moment. I don't know if the nerves will start to kick in tomorrow. It normally does. I have never had an interview where I was not nervous.

I am really enjoying listening to this song "Vertigo" by Groove Armada. I was recollecting the chill out music I listened to when

I was still living with my mother. For a split second, I was back in my mother's living room. How things have changed.

I have written quite a lot since July. I guess being at home during Covid has given me more opportunity to journal. It has helped me clear my mind and is therapeutic. It is surprising how much I can learn about myself from the random things I write about. During the time when I am writing, the thoughts seem almost meaningless. I write thoughts that are fleeting and mundane, but some thoughts are still relevant after many years.

28 September 2020

It is 9:24am. The morning of my government lawyer interview. My nerves are starting to kick in. I am starting to feel nervous. My heart is pounding just a little bit faster.

It is 10:35am. I am feeling nervous. I don't know how not to feel the nerves. How can I get rid of this feeling? I am feeling full blown nervousness. Remember when I was nervous during my OISC exam? What about the Level 2 IAAS accreditation exam? What about my interview with ABC? Was I nervous about my interview with JK? I think maybe the nerves started to kick around half hour before the interview. What about when I had to lead meetings or call a difficult client? Did I not get the same feeling? Yes, I did - even though I have nothing to worry about. Nerves, nerves, nerves. I just want to chill out. After this, I will try to book a massage.

It is about ten minutes before my interview. I guess I am feeling a bit more relaxed now. I think I have reached the stage where I just want to get it over and done with. I can't wait for it to be 3pm already. Just be yourself. Have a great time. Try to laugh at yourself.

It is 10:45pm. I had the interview. It took up a lot of my energy. I think I did ok in the first part but could have done better during the middle. I hope I was able to pick it back up at the end. In order to get through the interview, I was pretending like I don't want the job so I can feel cool and calm about it but at this stage, it is harder not to want it. In trying to achieve my goals, how do I forget I want it to avoid going insane, then try again if need be? I just feel like the rest of the day was blurry.

At least I am looking forward to going back to work tomorrow. Work now seems easy and comfortable in comparison. It is a good form of distraction.

29 September 2020

Following on the pressured interview from yesterday, I am glad to be doing something that I am familiar with. I feel less stressed. Because I don't have to prepare for interview, I am able to work overtime if need be. I am actually glad that I am back at work so I can feel distracted.

It is 10:45pm. Reading my journal from 2015, I realise that my enthusiasm for a legal career in my current field was probably at the highest during this time. It is hard to believe that I sincerely felt happy going to work and eagerly wanting to be the best lawyer in my field of law. The feeling of enthusiasm was so strong. Once I reached the point of qualifying as a lawyer, somehow, it is not how I imagined I would feel. Every time I dream of something, it never turns out how I expected it would. Perhaps I did not really know what I want as well as I thought or maybe I simply live to dream.

Going through the application process for the government lawyer role, I have built up the desire so strongly. It is possible I might not get it and I have no right to dream about getting the job nor imagining I am a government lawyer. I have no right to do this and I should not expect or feel any bit of entitlement towards it. There is a small part of me that wants to enjoy dreaming about getting the job, even if I don't get it, dreaming about it makes me feel good even though this could bring disappointment. I realise that dreaming about this dream in itself is what keeps me feeling alive.

Looking back to how much I desired my current position in this area of law, I am finally able to see the full picture – pixels and all that I never knew were there. Somehow, it makes me wonder – I want the government lawyer role so much now and if I do get it, will there be a day that I would not want the job anymore as I would be able to see the good, the bad and the ugly? Perhaps dreaming about it can keep my aspirations alive. Reading my journal from five years ago allows me to learn about myself. The writing at that time was so genuine and fitting then. Ironically, in those journals I wrote how much I had changed as a person and now reading those parts I realise how much I have again evolved. If my previous journal entries made comments about how un-believable the changes were, the difference from those moments of reflection to now is even more vast.

Reading back to my previous entries, my thoughts have certainly evolved and it is a learning process to understand the transition. Now, I have come to understand that although I write what is ac-curate for me now, it may not reflect the future me. It is almost certain that I will evolve but I do not know what kind of person I will become or what kind of aspirations I will have.

This journal is simply a record of pursuing my desired aim. It serves as a record to monitor my thoughts through the journey I have chosen for the future. Whatever happens from recording this journey, whether the goals transpire or not, is probably sec-ondary. It is more about finding out myself, how to deal with life and embarking on journey of growth from paralegal to qualifying as a lawyer and beyond. If you think you want it now, truly think about what else you are likely to want in the future as you evolve.

Perhaps dreaming keep my senses alive. Perhaps I need to wake up and enjoy what I have. Perhaps life should be enjoyed as it is, with little complications. Perhaps there does not have to be anything more to life but contentment. Perhaps the childhood dream of living a meaningful life by changing the world is so naïve, infantile and trivial. Perhaps life is simply to co-exist and make do with what we have to use at our advantage.

12. PATIENCE IS A VIRTUE

30 September 2020

If you think you know what you want, you will never actually know until you have it. It is only when you see your dreams in reality, in light of the good, the bad and the ugly that you realise dreams are merely happy delusions to get you through the journey of life.

I realised that my life may not have been better if I had a father present or if had been born into a wealthy family. I was able to reach my goal to qualify as a lawyer because of the strength I gained through hardship that I encountered and not despite of it, contrary to what I have always believed. The years spent in the market, commuting to school by waking at 4am and sleeping at midnight as a child meant that I was already training with the hours, stress and hardship of a lawyer during my early childhood years. As a child, my training was priceless. It cannot be bought, nor truly taught, but can only be what it has to be - experienced. This discovery has led me to reach a full circle in understanding my life. I no longer resented my father for throwing us in the dungeon of economic poverty to be eaten alive by a lion, for I fought the battle of poverty and also gained the strength of a lion.

2 October 2020

It is Friday, 10:15pm. I am going back on furlough from Wednesday. I have two more days of working. The initiations are down which means it is very possible that another round of redundancy can be taken.

4 October 2020

I am currently listening to a mass online. I feel sorry for others who are suffering, especially now during the pandemic. Here I am wishing for the role as a government lawyer when there are so many others with wishes probably relating to life and death. Viewed upon this perspective, my wish is senseless. It feels wrong for me to wish for a job when there are so many others with serious problems. I must always remember how blessed I truly am. This journey of becoming the person I want to be is perhaps about accepting who I am and being grateful for who I already am. Perhaps there is no need to reinvent the wheel by completely changing but rather working with the blessings I already have right now.

7 October 2020

First day back on furlough and I am absolutely loving life. I want to think about life generally. What do I want in 10 years' time? I would like for our mortgage to be paid off as much as possible.

I need a process for dealing with failures, rejections or things going wrong. I do not need to be the smartest, I just need to be smart enough. I do not need to be polished, as long as I am structured enough. Being mediocre is enough. Being me is enough. What I have is enough. My life is good enough.

13 October 2020

In the last four days, I have been doing things that I enjoy so no pressure of trying to be productive.

I met up with a friend, Jessica on Friday. On Saturday, I did some cleaning and tried shooting videos for You Tube. I just wanted to try the process of making a video and uploading this. On Sunday, I met up with my friend Venus. We had lunch and I felt sick afterwards. It was probably the food or it could be because I ate too quickly. Either way, I was put off eating red meat for a while. Yesterday, I did not do much but I cooked lentils. I also did yoga. I finished reading the book "Marshmallow Test". Today, I did some drawing using ink. Overall, I had a really good time.

13 November 2020

It is Friday, 12:53pm. It is my day off. I have been tidying up my drawers and other bits and bobs. Now I am chilling out with a coffee. I am looking more into how I can live my life in a simple way. By now, I have an idea of the things I like. I will try not to buy so many things. In a world where people want everything instantly, it is harder not to want things or desire to change ourselves. Simple. Make it easy for myself. Life does not have to be so complicated.

17 November 2020

This time two years ago, I woke up to prepare for my wedding. I want to rewind the time to that moment so I can engage more fully during the wedding. I was so nervous during the wedding I feel that it had all gone so quickly. Lesson learnt, be more present and try to engage with people during events.

21 November 2020

There is a chance I am going through a mid-life crisis. I have lost the meaning of life. I seem to have forgotten my purpose. The more I looked into it, the more it felt like I was going through it. I do not regret the route that I have taken and in fact I am proud of what I have achieved. I have pretty much obtained what I set out to achieve and for that I am glad. Now that I have qualified, I pretty much planned the rest of my life. I know how the rest of my life is likely to turn out. Is there anything else to the rest of my life? Would I have any regrets when I am 60 years old? Is there anything that I could have done right now that I would want to do when I am older? If I do not think about these things, time will pass by so quickly and I may find myself when I am 60 years old having some regrets of not being able to determine what I should have done sooner. I have been watching You Tube videos about the biggest regrets older people have. Some of it include: not pursuing goals, not spending time with family and friends, working too hard, not being true to self. I want to avoid all of these potential regrets by the time I reach 60 years old.

23 November 2020

I am trying to avoid over stimulating my brain. I think this might help with my insomnia. I started setting up my new laptop which is an Asus flipbook. The screen folds backwards so it can be used like a tablet. Normally I would be all over the laptop and I will be using it until midnight but because I am trying to cut down dopamine levels, I will continue it tomorrow.

24 November 2020

It is Tuesday and so far I am having an easy day at work. I hope this will continue.

Today, I invested some more money on Bitcoin. I want to see how much profit I can make in the next month or so. Last year, I invested in Bitcoin but as Covid19 happened, I was sceptical about the market so I held off some of my funds. There was uncertainty of the bearish market during the pandemic. Recently, the crypto market has started to pick up so I want to make the most of the hopefully bullish run in the next month. I also have other investments with general stocks and shares, mostly mutual funds in a separate account and these pay dividends directly to my bank account but I do not really look at these as I find the growth too slow. I find cryptos more interesting. I like the volatility of high risk and I try to trade around this.

I actually found out about Bitcoin through a guy I met whilst I was on holiday last year in November 2019. He said he wanted to retire in his 40s. I asked how he intends to do this and he said through Bitcoin. Once I tried it, I was hooked. At least this hobby is a good distraction for me to avoid feeling low. Luke has also started to invest in Bitcoin. We are officially a Bitcoin household.

25 November 2020

It turns out that my employer JK, will sublet our office so we are continuing to work from home. That is brilliant news! I would save money, almost like an instant pay rise. It is less likely that people would be made redundant. I am happy that I do not have to commute. This news has really cheered me up.

5 December 2020

I worked freelance at my second job. I was dealing with an existing client's renewal application. I did the initial work years ago. Looking back at the letter of advice and representations I did for this client, I have to admit my drafting was impeccable. Even I was impressed with the work I had done years earlier, when I should really be looking back thinking of improvements. I was incredibly passionate about what I did and it showed through my work. I can see that I left no stone unturned. My drafting then was like a legal sword that cut through the complex case of this client. I triggered every article I could invoke from the ECHR, all of the domestic rules and cases I could muster. I still remember how happy I was when the application was granted. Fast forward to a few years later, a more sobering situation as I prepared the extension. As this was an extension, it was going to be easy. I miss the passion but I do not miss the overall headache of Legal Aid Agency, including the pay.

Perhaps I take both roles for granted. I should remember that I am lucky. I have two jobs during this difficult time of pandemic. Both jobs are happy to give me work.

It is 10:25pm. I also managed to complete my personal admin. It is surprising that doing things are actually quicker than expected. For instance, I worried that completing SDLT form would be cumbersome but actually it was straightforward. Perhaps I should just do things without thinking so much to avoid worrying about them.

7 December 2020

It was busy today but I quite enjoyed it. I guess I like being busy. I have a headache from looking at the screen for too long though.

It is now 10pm. I reviewed my goals from last year and note that

I have achieved a few of my goals but a large part remains incomplete. I prefer not to dwell on what I have not achieved and would rather focus on the positive side of things. I surprised myself that I was able to have vegetarian days. I am pleased with this progress and I want to increase my vegetarian days to four days a week. I was also able to arrange renovation of the new house.

I should not be so hard on myself. Right now, I feel like I am not even trying to achieve my future goals. Perhaps I should focus on how to obtain some voluntary experience in chambers to get advocacy experience. Let me think about how I can move forward with my goals.

8 December 2020

I was thinking of signing up to serve as a Magistrate and volunteer at Further Representations Unit. I can try and do this during my spare time. The hardest part is trying to find the spare time. If I am able to get this experience, I would learn about criminal law and employment law. I would learn the skills of how to judge situations and also develop my advocacy skills. I need to think long and hard about this as signing up is easy. Starting and maintaining the part, that is difficult.

13 December 2020

I thought about my goals. I looked at the spreadsheet I made several years ago listing down goals I wanted to achieve. I assessed that becoming a judge and a Solicitor Advocate (including participating in three landmark cases) are probably the most difficult. I looked at my list closely. It dawned on me that my goal of becoming a judge is not in fact specific to a particular judge. Theoretically, it can be a Magistrate as it does not specify it has to be a paid judge. If I manage to volunteer as a Magistrate, then I guess I should be able to cross off this goal.

Hard to believe but for 2021, I actually want to live a slow life carrying out work that I love and bring me joy in line with my future goals. Perhaps I should consider working part time. How would I feel about taking a pay cut if I have reduced hours? Will I regret it? Should I just stick it out in my field, try to master it as much as possible and eventually get a higher salary? That is the traditional route of a lawyer. How would I feel if people that I know will all earn more than me? Would I be comfortable with that? I am not in desperate need for money so I am lucky in that regard. Do I have an aversion to earning more money? Do I attach more money to more responsibilities? Perhaps. If I work in the next 20 years when I am in my 50s, trying to achieve more and more money switching from one firm to another firm, I feel that the rest of my life would be boring with very little prospect of trying to achieve my outstanding goals. Is it just a matter of trying to change my mindset?

Why is that I have been working so hard so I can be in this position (and I would have loved to be in this position) but now that it is there, I take my life for granted? Why can't I just try to master this field, soldier on and become one of the best in the field rather than fiddling with other areas that I may or may not specialise in the future? What is it about trying to get through the most difficult parts that I enjoy but once the majority of the goal is complete and there is certainty as to the results, I somehow find the rest mundane. Although I thrive in difficult and under resourced environment, must I put myself back to such situations in order to thrive?

Why am I not able to bring out the best in myself when things are going so perfectly well for me? In my romanticised vision of success, I have always envisaged hard work as part of it. But must success always be hard work? Can't I just embrace the easy road to success? Am I simply unable to enjoy a comfortable life, having strived relentlessly since childhood to be out of perpetual discomfort? Is it a matter of being ungrateful, having forgotten the world of poverty once left behind? Am I suffering from an honour roll hangover or a mid-life crisis? Is it an expectation that achievements should be reached at a steady growth? Am I simply taking an inventory and calculating what else I can do as a way to brainstorm how great my life could possibly be? After all of this analysis, I am still at loss as to what I should do. I will proceed with trying to sign up as a Magistrate.

14 December 2020

I had a vision of not having to work and it was pure bliss. Back to the real world.

15 December 2020

Choices. Am I unfulfilled because I have too many choices?

16 December 2020

Just before 9am. I am about to embark on another day's work. Already a lot of emails even before I start. I will try my best to get through them.

17 December 2020

I received an email today confirming I passed the interview stage for the government lawyer role. The next step would be to go through references and DBS check. I am over the moon. I am so incredibly happy. I cannot believe that I was able to get through.

22 December 2020

I am so thrilled about getting the government lawyer role. I still have to go through pre-employment checks but I still feel so happy.

I have a great opportunity to be a lawyer for the government and make an impact to society. I can make a difference. My favourite quote is this:

"...I will do right to all manner of people after the laws and usages of this realm, without fear or favour, affection or ill will."

I shall be guided by this principle. I am going to be a lawyer advising the government at a time like no other with Brexit and

Covid19. It is a great title with an even greater responsibility. I will do everything in my power in accordance with the law to help the government in helping the country.

Printed in Great Britain
by Amazon